MILTON KEYNES

BUCKINGHAM   BLETCHLEY   LEIGHT

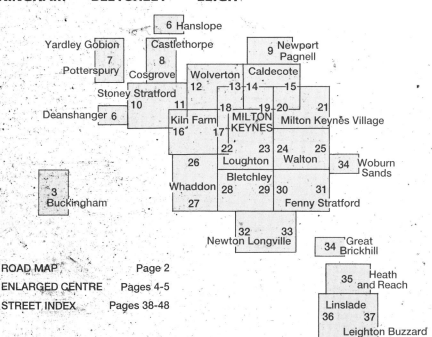

6 Hanslope

Yardley Gobion   Castlethorpe   9 Newport Pagnell

7   8

Potterspury   Cosgrove   Wolverton   Caldecote

12   13-14   15

Stoney Stratford

10   11   18   19-20   21

Deanshanger 6   Kiln Farm   MILTON   Milton Keynes Village

16   17 KEYNES

22   23 24   25

26   Loughton   Walton   34 Woburn Sands

Bletchley

Whaddon   28   29 30   31

3   27   Fenny Stratford

Buckingham

32   33

Newton Longville   34 Great Brickhill

ROAD MAP   Page 2

ENLARGED CENTRE   Pages 4-5   35 Heath and Reach

STREET INDEX   Pages 38-48

Linslade

36   37

Leighton Buzzard

Every effort has been made to verify the accuracy of information in this book but the publishers cannot accept responsibility for expenses or loss caused by any error or omission. Information that will be of assistance to the user of the maps will be welcomed.

The representation of a road, track or footpath on the maps in this atlas is no evidence of the existence of a right of way.

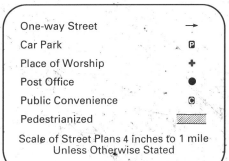

One-way Street	→
Car Park	🄿
Place of Worship	✛
Post Office	●
Public Convenience	🄲
Pedestrianized	▨

Scale of Street Plans 4 inches to 1 mile
Unless Otherwise Stated

Street plans prepared and published by ESTATE PUBLICATIONS, Bridewell House, TENTERDEN, KENT, and based upon the ORDNANCE SURVEY mapping with the permission of The Controller of H. M. Stationery Office.

The publishers acknowledge the co-operation of the local authorities of towns represented in this atlas.

© Estate Publications 521 B   ISBN 0 86084 969 4   © Crown Copyright 398713

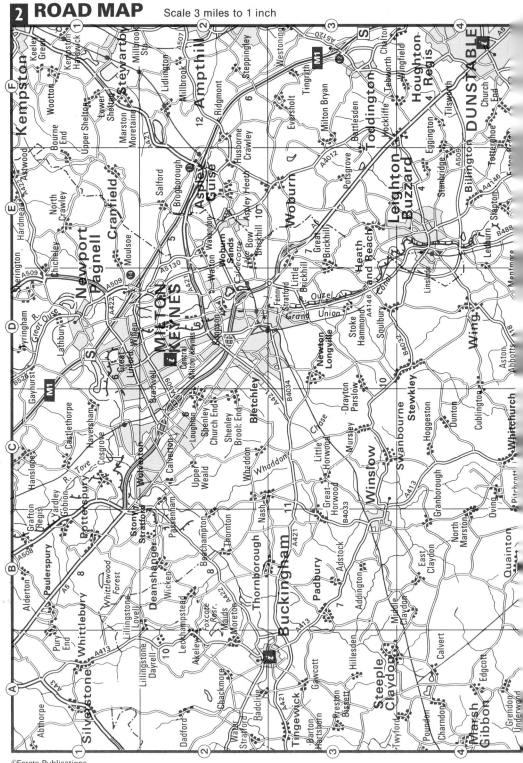

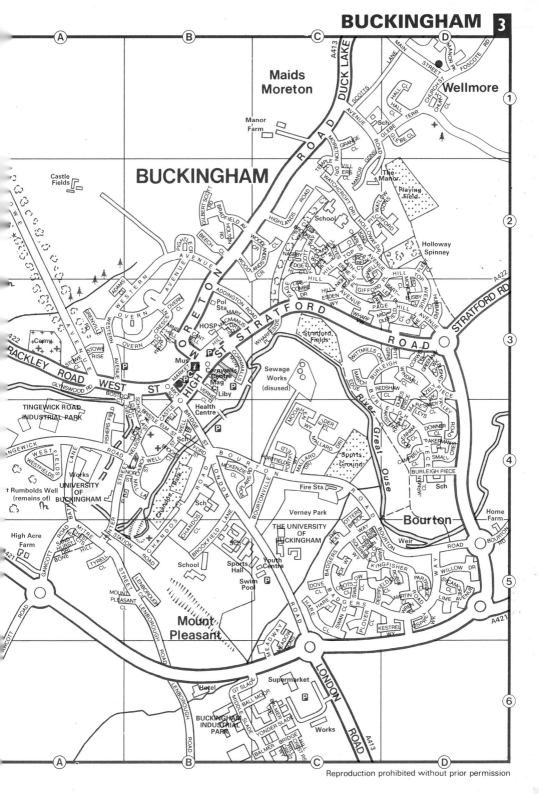

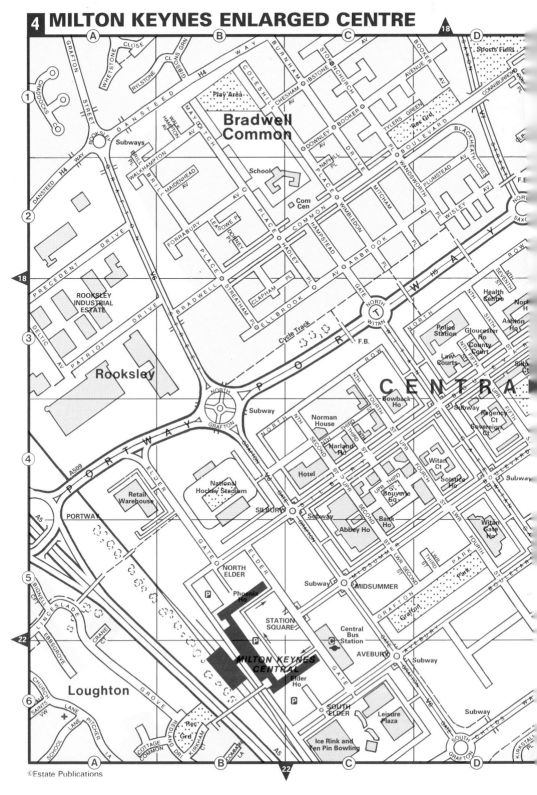

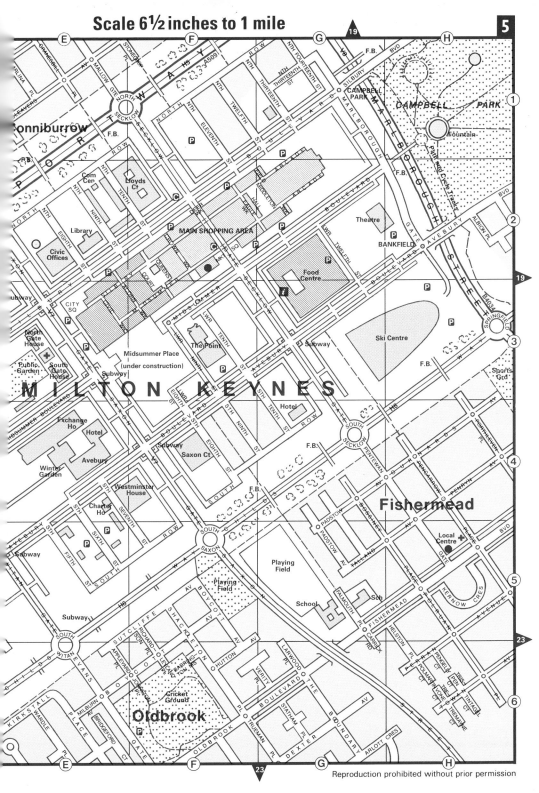

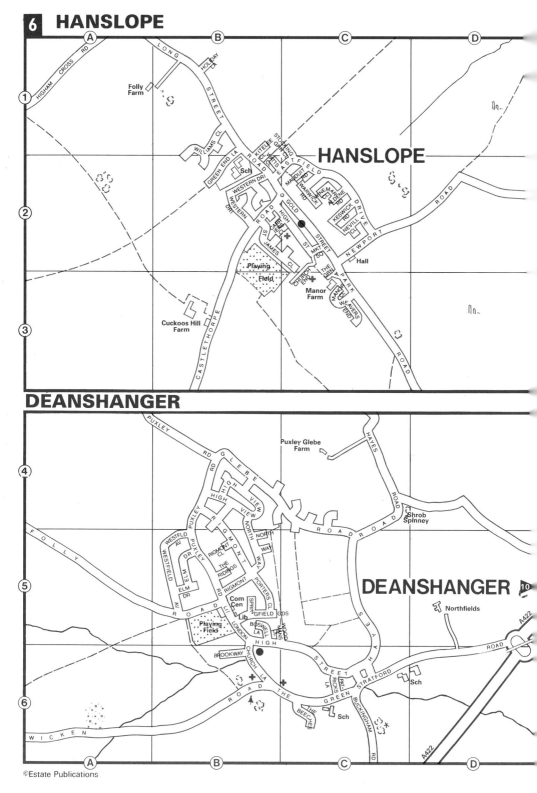

HANSLOPE

Folly Farm

HIGHAM CROSS RD

LONG STREET

HOLIDAY LA

WILLIAMS CL

GREEN END LA

Sch

WESTERN DRIVE

WESTERN DRI

KITELEE CL

STOCKING GREEN CL

STOCKFIELD ROAD

EASTFIELD

MALDUIT RD

WARWICK RD

NEW RD

CLARKE RD

ALDENE RD

KESWICK RD

NEVILL CL

HIGH ST

GOLD ST

CHURCH END

ST JAMES CL

CASTLETHORPE

Playing Field

Cuckoos Hill Farm

STREET

MKT SQ

THE GREEN

Manor Farm

MANOR CL

PARK

WEAVERS END

Hall

NEWPORT ROAD

DRIVE

ROAD

DEANSHANGER

PUXLEY RD

GLEBE RD

Puxley Glebe Farm

HAYES ROAD

HIGH VIEW

HIGH VIEW

NORTH VIEW

PUXLEY RD

RIGMONT CL

WESTFLD AV

WESTFIELD

ELM DR

PUXLEY DR

ELM DR

THE RIDINGS

RIGMONT

NORTH WAY

PORTERS CL

ROAD

ROAD

Shrob Spinney

FOLLY ROAD

Com Cen

Lib

SPRINGFIELD

GDS

Playing Field

BOSWELL LA

LONDON RD

CHURCH LA

BROOKWAY

HIGH STREET

THE GREEN

RICKS PAS

STRATFORD RD

Northfields

Sch

Sch

Sch

BUCKINGHAM RD

THE BEECHES

WICKEN

ROAD

A422

A422 ROAD

10

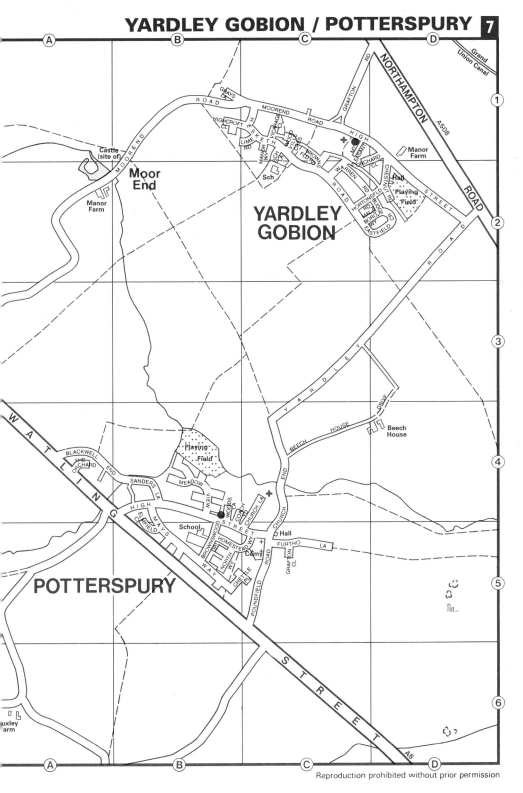

Grand
Union Canal

GRAYS CL

ROAD

MOOREND ROAD

HIGHCROFT CL

HESKETH

VICARAGE CL

MANOR WY

SCH

LIME RD

WOODS CL

DUNS... CL

BROWNS CL

NORTHAMPTON

GRAFTON

HIGH

STREET

A508

ROAD

Castle
(site of)

Manor
Farm

**Moor
End**

Sch

ORCHARD CL

WARREN

CHESTNUT RD

Manor
Farm

Hall

Playing
'Field'

ROAD

HORTONSFLD RD

HALL...

BOBOLE...

EASTFIELD

**YARDLEY
GOBION**

ROAD

YARDLEY

BEECH HOUSE

BLUE

Beech
House

WATLING

BLACKWELL
END

THE
ORCHARD

SANDERS LA

HIGH

MAYS CL

ELMFIELD

MEADOW
VIEW

Playing
'Field'

WOODS LA

COACH

CHURCH LA

BROWNSWOOD

STREET

School

NORTH WY

HOMESTEAD WY

Cemy

CHETTLE

ROAD

Hall

CHURCH

END

FURTHO LA

GRAFTON CL

POUNDFIELD

STREET

POTTERSPURY

uxley
arm

A5

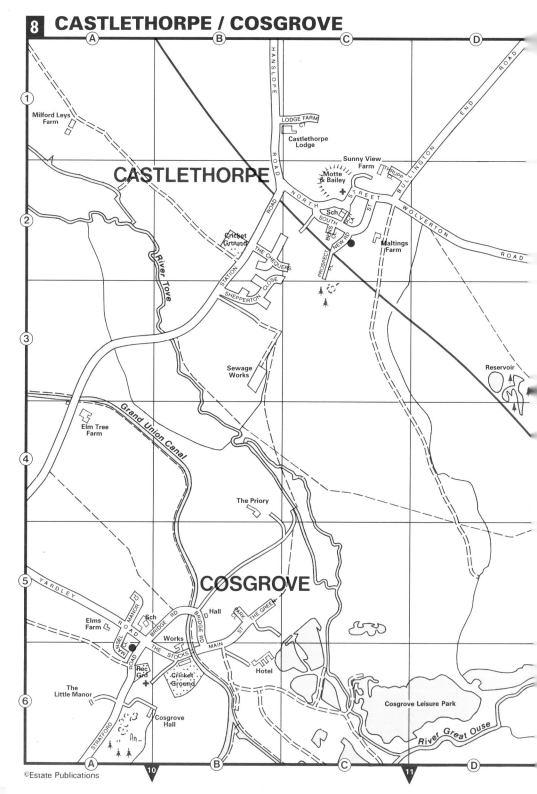

CASTLETHORPE

COSGROVE

Milford Leys Farm

LODGE FARM

Castlethorpe Lodge

Sunny View Farm

THRUPP CL

Motte & Bailey

Sch

Maltings Farm

Cricket Ground

THE CHEQUERS

STATION

SHEPPERTON

CLOSE

River Tove

HANSLOPE ROAD

NORTH STREET

SOUTH

BERS CL

PROSPECT PL

NEW RD

WOLVERTON ROAD

LINGTON

END ROAD

Sewage Works

Reservoir

Grand Union Canal

Elm Tree Farm

The Priory

YARDLEY

Elms Farm

MANSEL ROAD

MANOR CL

Sch

Hall

PARK ST

THE GREEN

BRIDGE RD

BRIDGE RD

MAIN

Works

THE STOCKS

Hotel

Rec Grd

Cricket Ground

The Little Manor

Cosgrove Hall

STRATFORD

Cosgrove Leisure Park

River Great Ouse

10   11

A   B   C   D

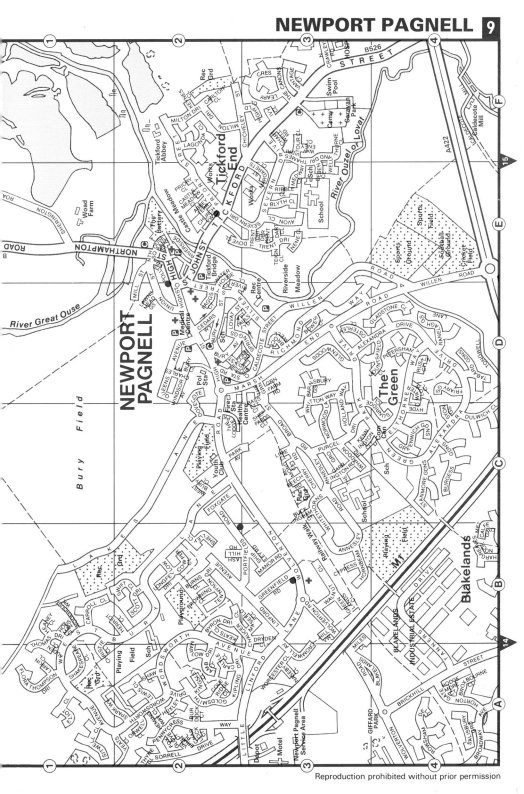

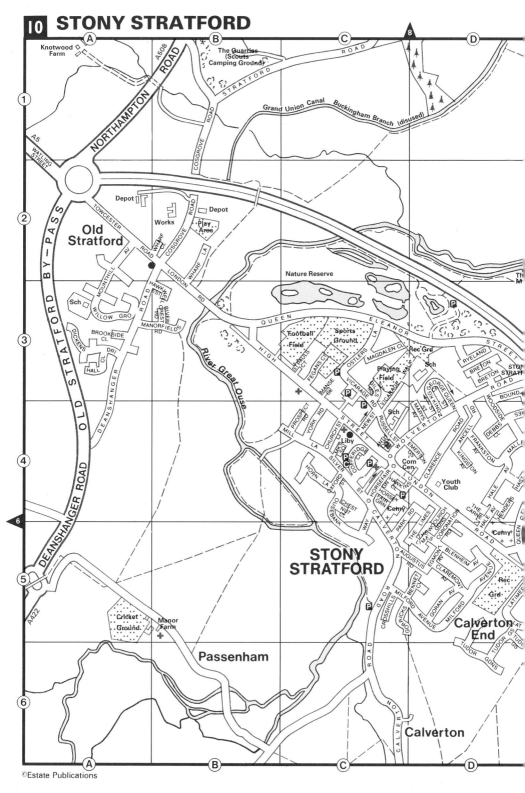

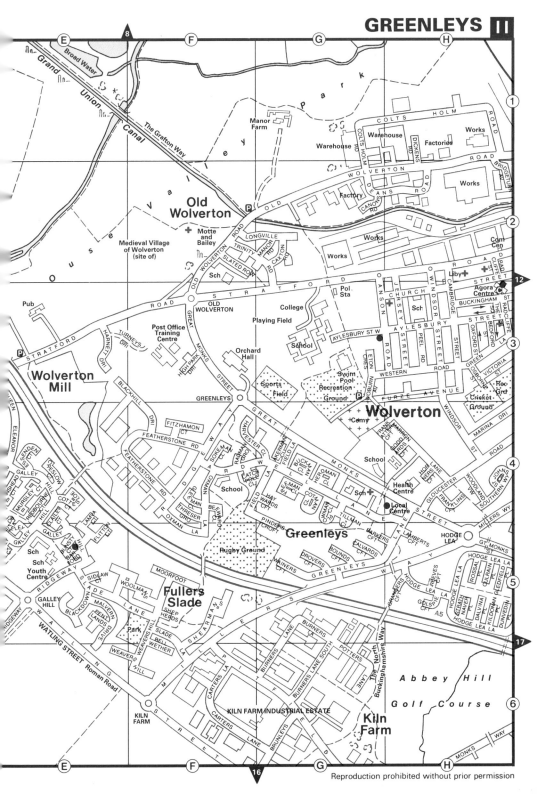

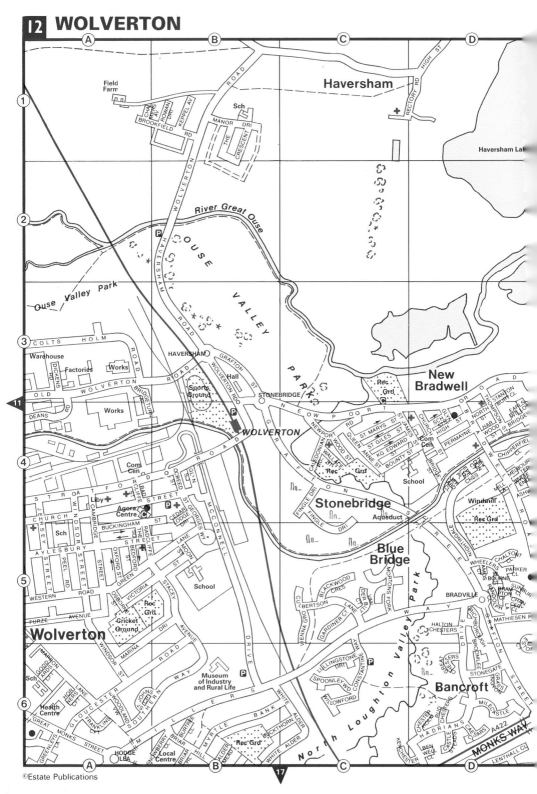

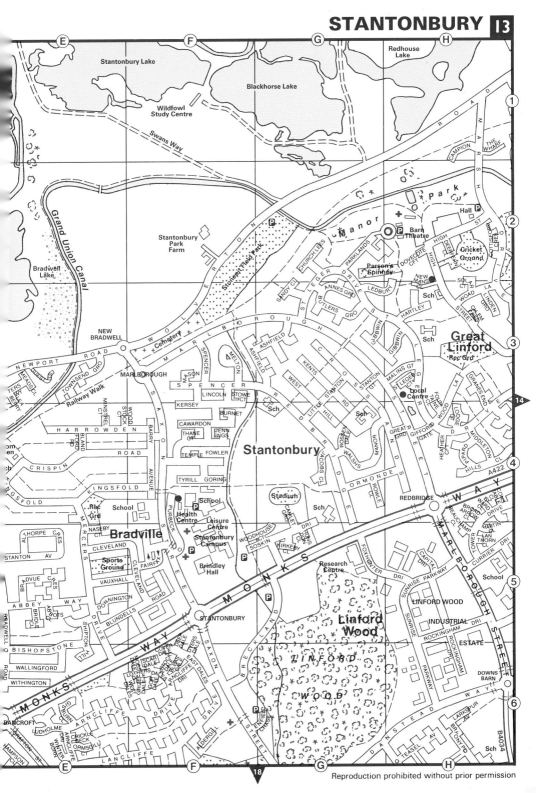

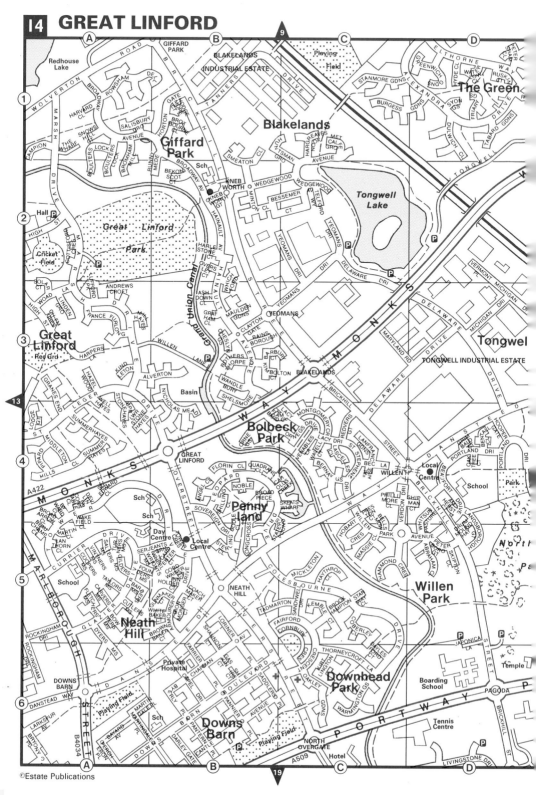

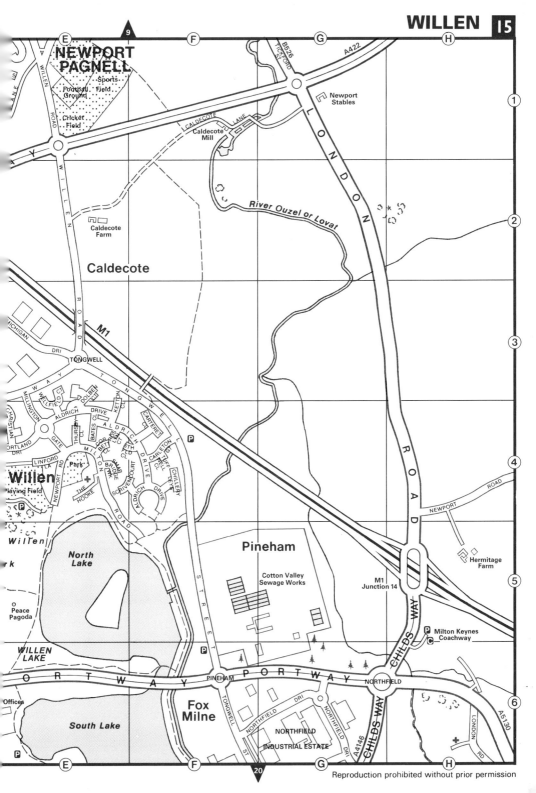

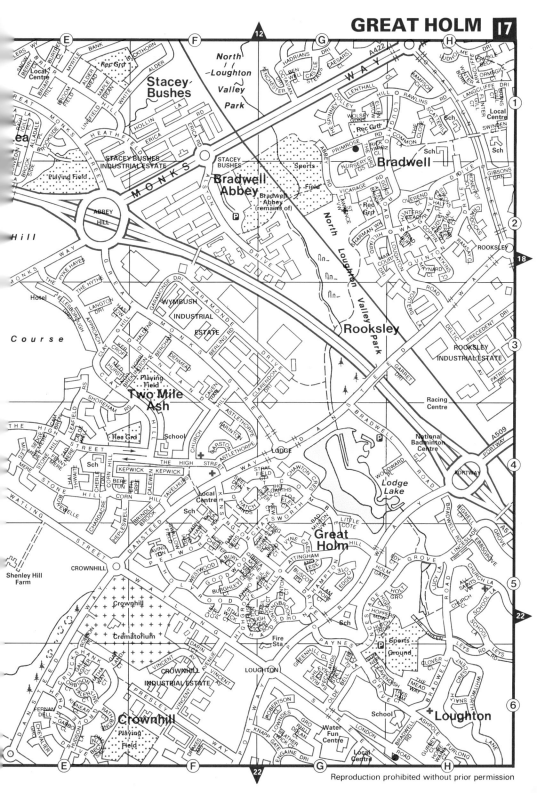

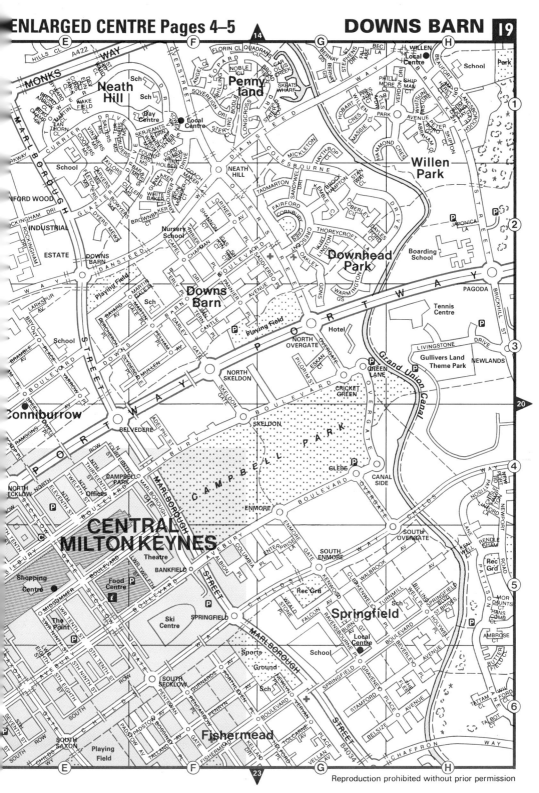

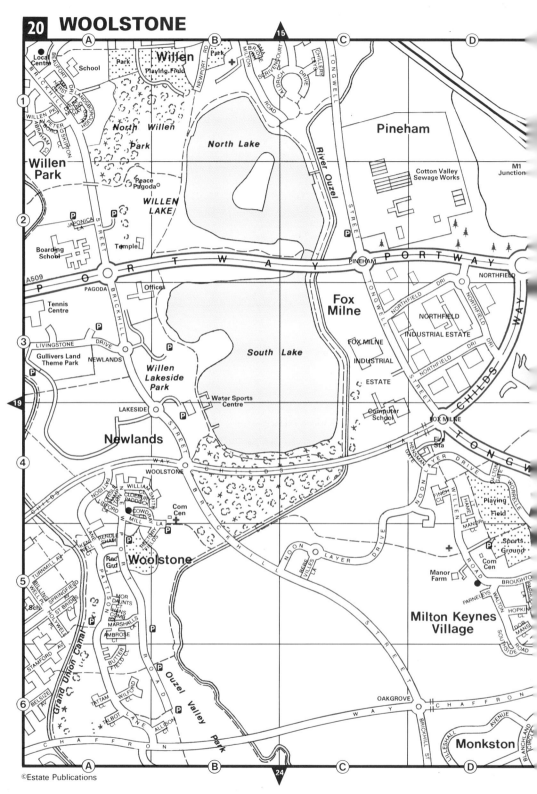

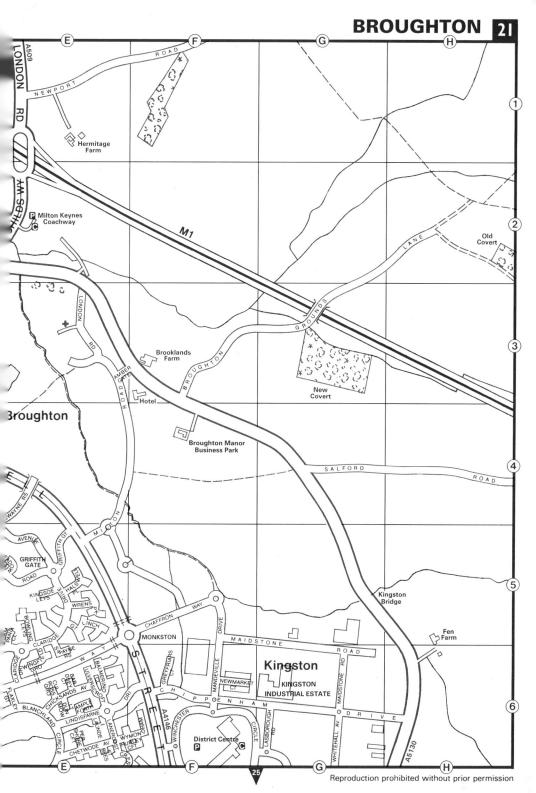

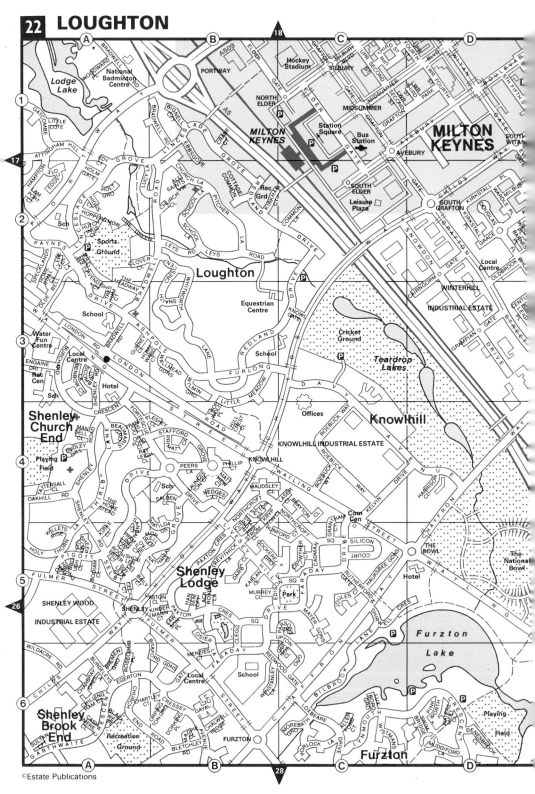

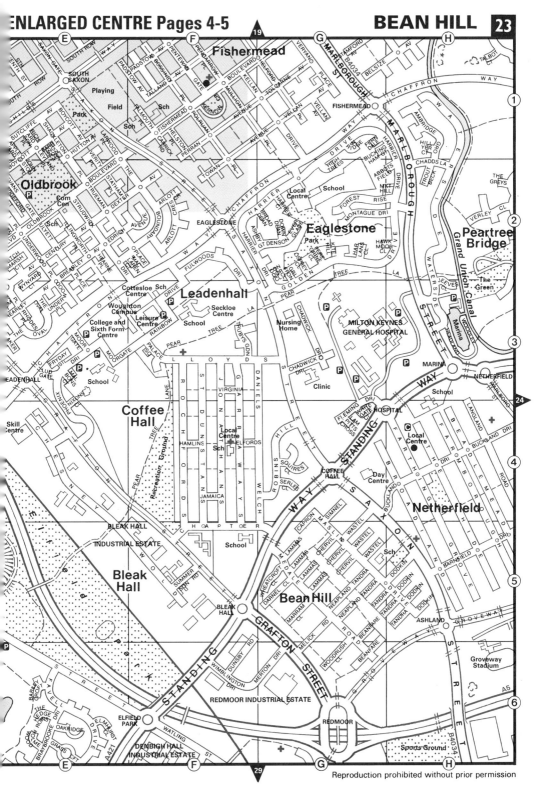

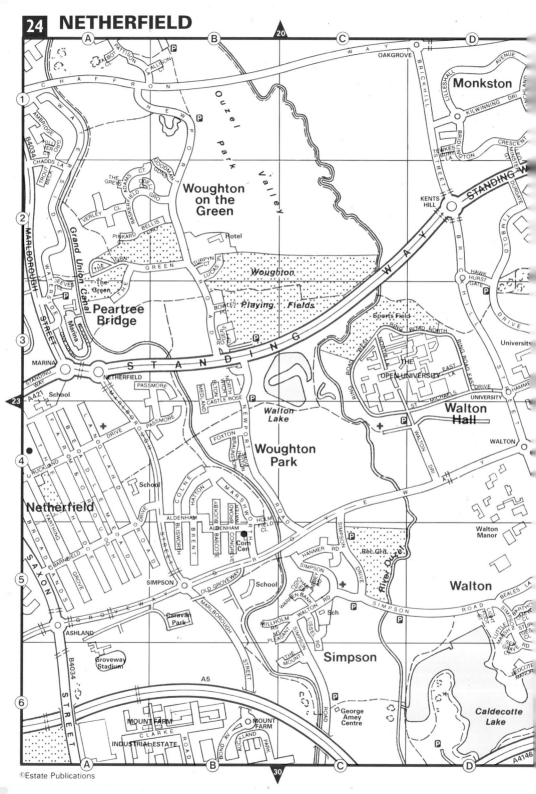

Monkston

Woughton on the Green

Ouzel Park Valley

Woughton Playing Fields

Peartree Bridge

Grand Union Canal

Hotel

The Green

Kents Hill

Sports Field

THE OPEN UNIVERSITY

Walton Hall

STANDING WAY

University

Hawkhurst Gate

MARINA

NETHERFIELD

School

PASSMORE

Walton Lake

Woughton Park

Walton

Netherfield

School

Simpson

Com Cen

School

Caravan Park

ASHLAND

Groveway Stadium

Warren Bank

Millholm

Mt Pleasant

Sch

Walton Manor

Rec. Grd.

River Ouzel

Simpson

George Amey Centre

Caldecotte Lake

MOUNT FARM

INDUSTRIAL ESTATE

MOUNT FARM

A5

A4146

B4034

A421

23

20

30

©Estate Publications

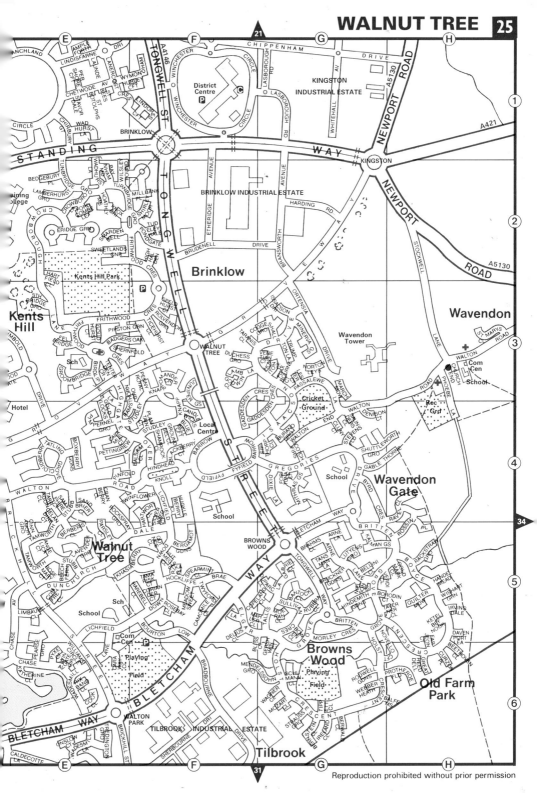

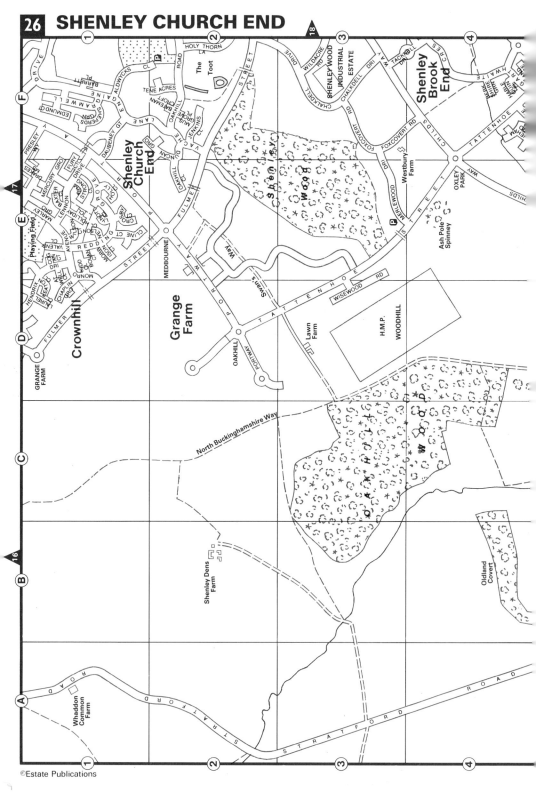

Shenley Church End

Shenley Brook End

Crownhill

Grange Farm

SHENLEY WOOD INDUSTRIAL ESTATE

Shenley Wood

The Toot

Holy Thorn La

Westbury Farm

Ash Pole Spinney

OXLEY PARK

Lawn Farm

H.M.P. WOODHILL

OAKHILL WOOD

North Buckinghamshire Way

Shenley Dens Farm

Oldland Covert

Whaddon Common Farm

STRATFORD ROAD

GRANGE FARM

Playing Field

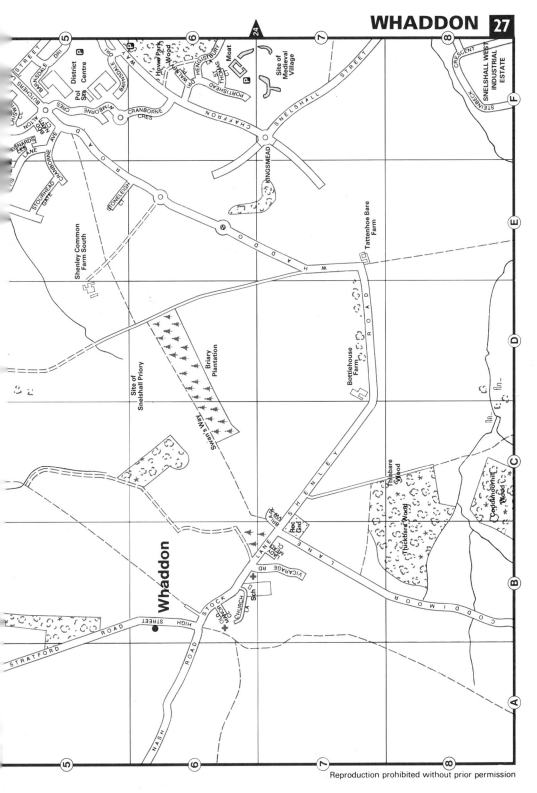

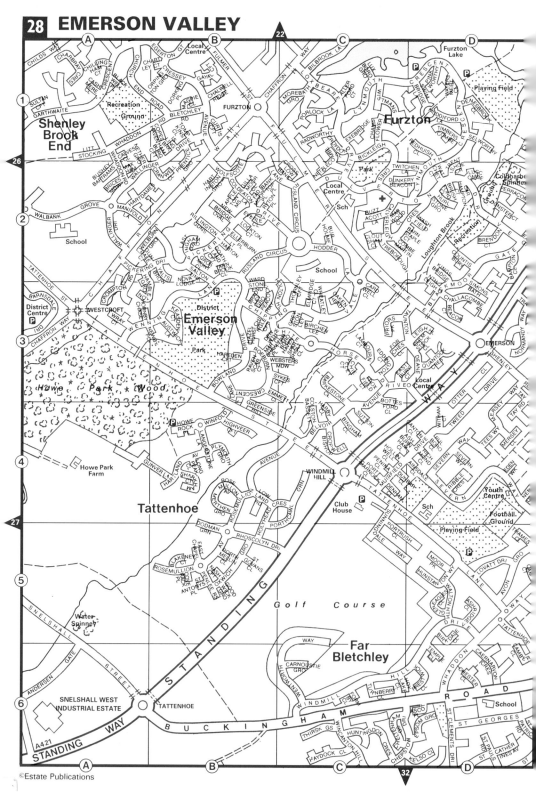

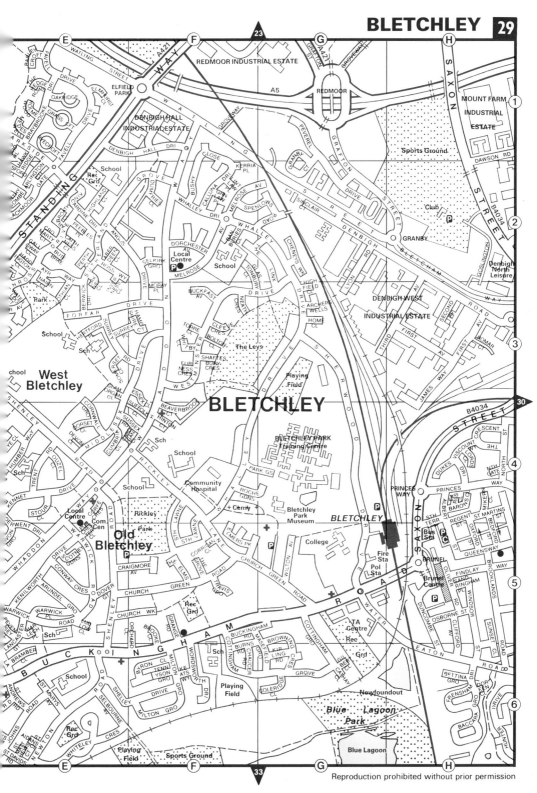

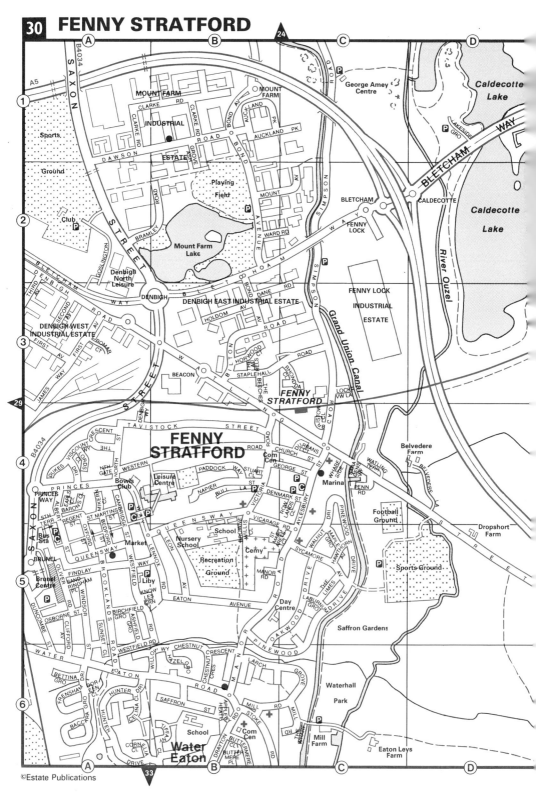

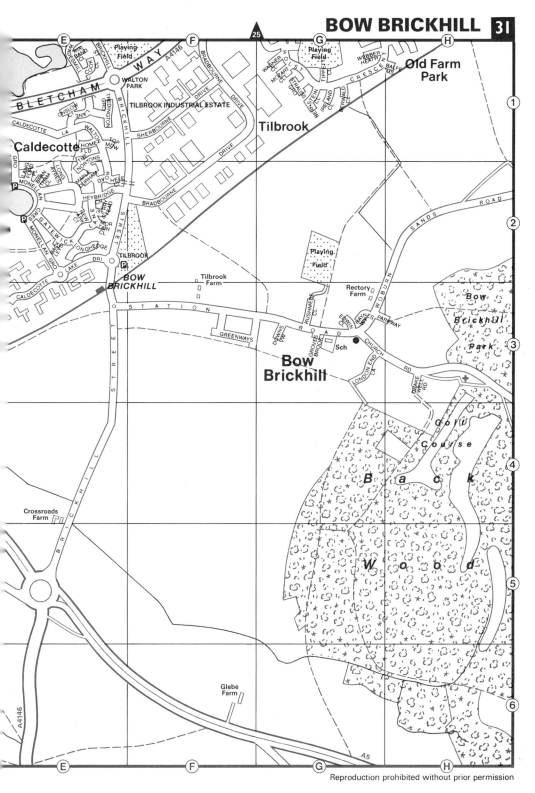

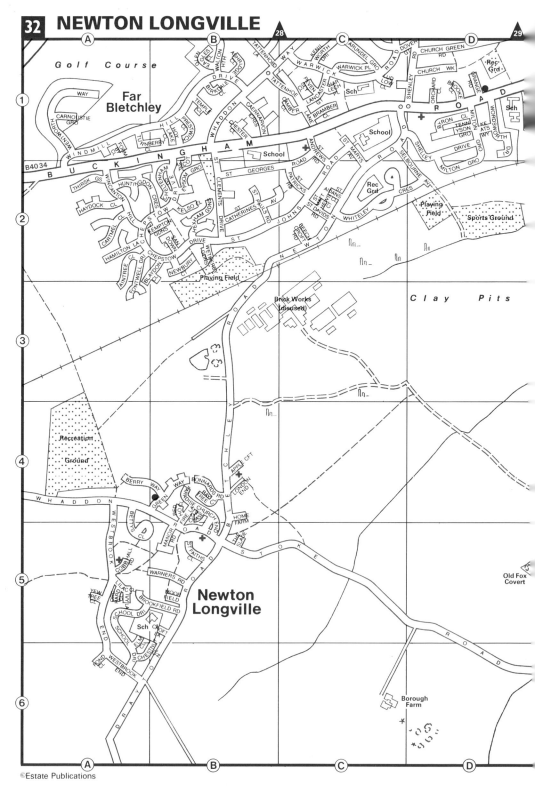

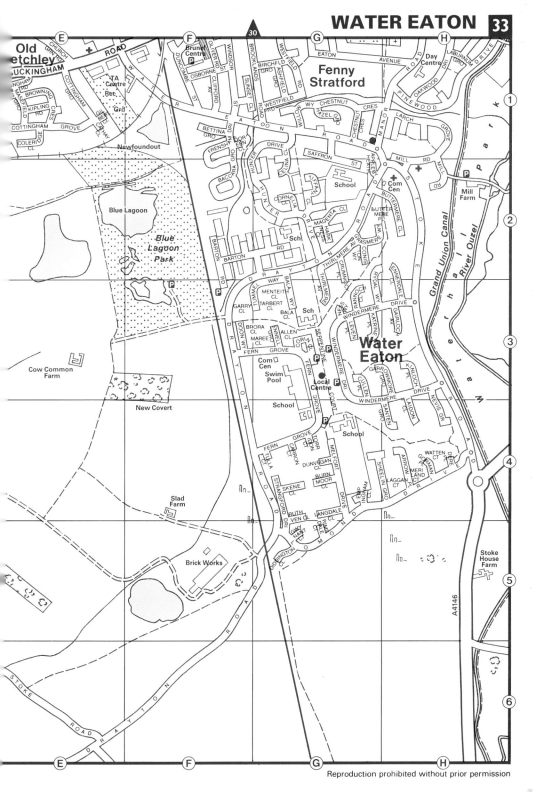

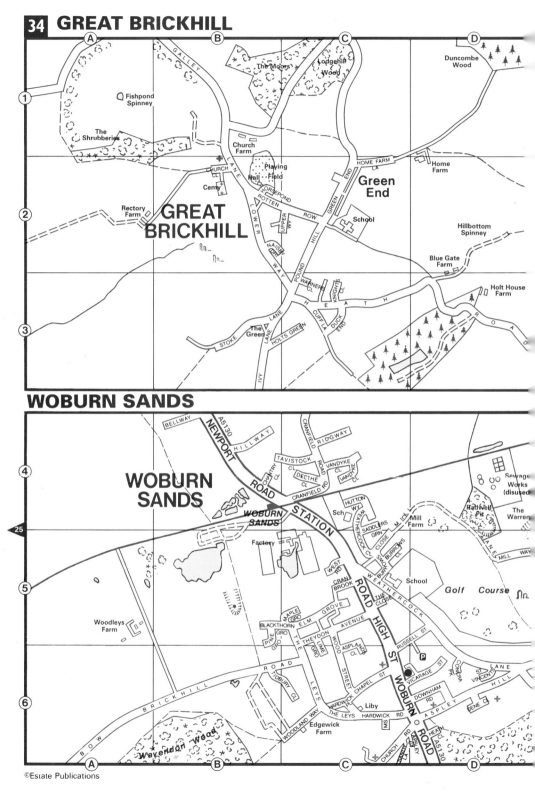

GREAT BRICKHILL

Green End

WOBURN SANDS

WOBURN SANDS

©Estate Publications

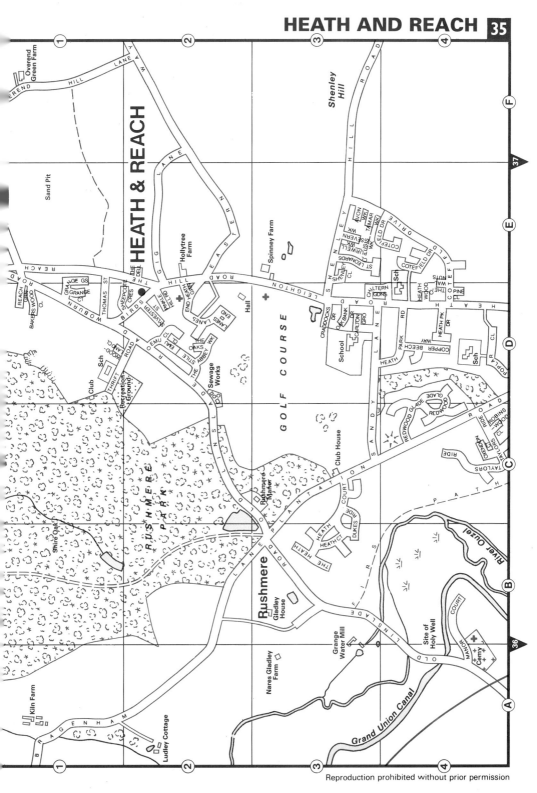

The Index includes some names for which there is insufficient space on the maps. These names are preceded by an * and are followed by the nearest adjoining thoroughfare.

Eastern Way. LU7	35 E2	Blakedown Rd. LU7	36 A4
Emu Clo. LU7	35 D2	Bossard Ct. LU7	37 E3
Firs Path. LU7	35 B3	Bossington La. LU7	36 D3
Gig La. LU7	35 E2	Bramble Clo. LU7	37 G4
Grange Ct. LU7	35 D1	Bridge St. LU7	36 D4
Grange Gdns. LU7	35 D1	Broadrush Grn. LU7	36 C3
Heath Ct. LU7	35 B3	Brook St. LU7	37 G3
Heath Grn. LU7	35 D2	Brooklands. LU7	37 F4
Heath Park Dri. LU7	35 D4	Brooklands Dri. LU7	37 F4
Heath Park Rd. LU7	35 D4	Brookside Walk. LU7	37 G3
Heath Rd. LU7	35 D4	Broomhills Rd. LU7	37 E1
Heathwood Clo. LU7	35 D4	Browns Lea. LU7	37 G4
Isis Walk. LU7	35 E3	Bunkers La. LU7	36 B4
Lanes End. LU7	35 D2	By-Pass. LU7	36 A6
Leighton Rd. LU7	35 D3	Calder Gdns. LU7	36 A3
Manor Ct. LU7	35 A4	Camberton Rd. LU7	36 C5
Oakbank Dri. LU7	35 D3	Capshill Av. LU7	37 G3
Old Linslade Rd. LU7	35 A4	Carina Dri. LU7	37 G3
Overend Hill La. LU7	35 F1	Carnation Clo. LU7	37 E2
Oxendon Ct. LU7	35 C4	Carron Clo. LU7	36 A4
Pine Clo. LU7	35 D4	Cedars Way. LU7	36 C5
Pinkle Hill Rd. LU7	35 D2	Centauri Clo. LU7	37 G3
Plantation Rd. LU7	35 C3	Cetus Cres. LU7	37 G3
Poplar Clo. LU7	35 D4	Chamberlains Gdns. LU7	37 E1
Purwell Walk. LU7	35 E3	Chapel Path. LU7	37 E3
Reach Grn. LU7	35 D1	Chartmoor Rd. LU7	37 E6
Redwood Glade. LU7	35 C4	Chelsea Grn. LU7	36 B4
Robinswood Clo. LU7	35 C4	Cherry Ct. LU7	37 H4
St Leonards Clo. LU7	35 E3	Cherry Ct Way. LU7	37 H4
Sandy La. LU7	35 C3	Cherrycourt Way Ind Est. LU7	37 H4
Severn Walk. LU7	35 E3	Chestnut Hill. LU7	36 B2
Sheepcote Cres. LU7	35 D2	Chestnut Rise. LU7	36 B2
Shenley Clo. LU7	35 E3	Cheviot Clo. LU7	36 A2
Shenley Hill Rd. LU7	35 D3	Chiltern Trading Est. LU7	37 E5
Sylvester St. LU7	35 D2	Church Av. LU7	37 E4
Tamar Walk. LU7	35 E3	Church Rd. LU7	36 C4
Taylors Ride. LU7	35 C4	Church Sq. LU7	37 E4
The Dell. LU7	35 E2	Church St. LU7	37 E3
The Heath. LU7	35 B3	Church View Ct. LU7	36 C4
The Oaks. LU7	35 D2	Churchill Rd. LU7	37 F2
The Reach. LU7	35 D2	Clarence Rd. LU7	37 E2
The Stile. LU7	35 D2	Cleveland Dri. LU7	36 A2
The Walnuts. LU7	35 D4	Clipstone Cres. LU7	37 G3
Thomas St. LU7	35 D1	Columba Dri. LU7	37 G2
Thrift Rd. LU7	35 D1	Commerce Way. LU7	37 H5
Woburn Rd. LU7	35 D1	Coniston Rd. LU7	36 A4
Woodland Clo. LU7	35 D1	Corbet Ride. LU7	36 C3

LEIGHTON BUZZARD

		Corbet Sq. LU7	36 C2
		Cotswold Dri. LU7	36 A3
		Creran Walk. LU7	36 A3
		Crossway. LU7	37 G4
		Croxley Ct. LU7	36 D3
Acacia Clo. LU7	37 H4	Cutlers Way. LU7	37 F4
Adams Bottom. LU7	37 E1	Cygnus Dri. LU7	37 H3
Adastral Av. LU7	37 H5	Danes Way. LU7	37 G3
Albany Rd. LU7	37 F4	Delamere Gdns. LU7	36 A4
Alexandra Ct. LU7	36 D2	Derwent Rd. LU7	36 A3
Almond Rd. LU7	37 G2	Digby Rd. LU7	37 E2
Alwins Field. LU7	36 B2	Dingle Dell. LU7	37 E1
Appenine Way. LU7	37 G3	Doggett St. LU7	37 E3
Apple Tree Clo. LU7	36 B4	Dove Tree Rd. LU7	37 G2
Aquila Rd. LU7	37 H3	Drivers Clo. LU7	37 H3
Aries Ct. LU7	37 G3	Dudley St. LU7	37 E4
Ascot Dri. LU7	36 B4	Dulverton Ct. LU7	36 A3
Ash Grn. LU7	37 E2	Duncombe Dri. LU7	37 E4
Ashburnham Cres. LU7	36 C5	Durrell Clo. LU7	36 C3
Ashlong Clo. LU7	37 G4	East St. LU7	37 E3
Ashwell St. LU7	37 E3	Eden Way. LU7	36 A3
Atterbury Av. LU7	37 F3	Edward St. LU7	37 E3
Baker St. LU7	37 E3	Ennerdale Ct. LU7	36 B3
Barley Corn Clo. LU7	37 H3	Enterprise Way. LU7	37 E5
Barnabas Rd. LU7	36 B4	Epsom Clo. LU7	36 B4
Basildon Ct. LU7	36 D3	Fallow Field. LU7	37 G4
Bassett Rd. LU7	36 D4	Faulkners Way. LU7	36 D3
Beaudesert. LU7	37 E3	Finch Cres. LU7	36 C5
Bedford St. LU7	37 E3	Firbank Ct. LU7	37 E6
Beech Gro. LU7	36 C3	Firbank Way. LU7	37 E6
Bell Alley. LU7	37 E4	Firs Path. LU7	37 E1
Bewdley Dri. LU7	36 A4	Friday St. LU7	37 E4
Bideford Ct. LU7	36 A2	Fyne Dri. LU7	36 A3
Bideford Grn. LU7	36 B2	Garden Hedge. LU7	37 E3
Billington Ct. LU7	37 F5	Garden Leys. LU7	37 G4
Billington Rd. LU7	37 F5	Gemini Clo. LU7	37 H2

George St. LU7	37 F3	Meadow Way. LU7	37 H3
Globe La. LU7	36 C1	Meadway. LU7	37 G2
Golden Riddy. LU7	36 C3	Melfort Dri. LU7	36 A4
Grange Clo. LU7	36 C4	Mentmore Gdns. LU7	36 C5
Grasmere Way. LU7	36 B3	Mentmore Rd. LU7	36 C5
Greaves Way. LU7	37 H5	Mercury Way. LU7	37 H3
Greaves Way Ind Est. LU7	37 G5	Merlins Ct. LU7	37 E3
Greenhill. LU7	37 E1	Middle Grn. LU7	37 G3
Greenlands. LU7	37 G2	Midway. LU7	37 G4
Griboll Clo. LU7	36 A4	Milebush. LU7	36 B2
Grove Pl. LU7	37 E4	Miles Av. LU7	37 F3
Grove Rd. LU7	37 E4	Miletree Ct. LU7	37 F2
*Grovebury Mews, Grovebury Rd. LU7	37 E6	Mill Rd. LU7	37 E3
Grovebury Pl. LU7	37 E5	Millbank. LU7	36 D3
Grovebury Rd. LU7	37 E6	Millers Clo. LU7	37 H3
Hamilton Ct. LU7	37 E3	Millstream Way. LU7	36 D3
Hanover Ct. LU7	36 B3	Montgomery Clo. LU7	37 F2
Harcourt Clo. LU7	36 D3	Morar Clo. LU7	36 A3
Harmony Row. LU7	37 H5	Mountbatten Gdns. LU7	37 F2
Harrow Rd. LU7	37 F4	Mowbray Dri. LU7	36 B3
Hartwell Cres. LU7	37 F4	Nebular Ct. LU7	37 G3
Hartwell Gro. LU7	37 E4	Nelson Rd. LU7	37 F2
Harvester Ct. LU7	37 H3	Neptune Gdns. LU7	37 G3
Hawthorne Clo. LU7	36 C3	Nevis Clo. LU7	36 A4
Heath Rd. LU7	37 E2	New Rd. LU7	36 C4
Hercules Clo. LU7	37 G3	Newman Way. LU7	37 F3
High Croft. LU7	37 G5	North Star Dri. LU7	37 G3
High St. LU7	37 E4	North St. LU7	37 E3
Highfield Rd. LU7	37 G4	Northcourt. LU7	37 E2
Hillside Rd. LU7	37 E1	Oakley Grn. LU7	37 F2
Himley Grn. LU7	36 B4	Oatfield Gdns. LU7	37 H3
Hinton Clo. LU7	37 G4	Old Chapel Mews. LU7	37 E4
Hockliffe Rd. LU7	37 F3	Old Linslade Rd. LU7	36 B1
Hockliffe St. LU7	37 E3	Old Rd. LU7	36 C4
Hornbeam Clo. LU7	37 G2	Omega Ct. LU7	37 G3
Hydrus Dri. LU7	37 H2	Orchard Dri. LU7	36 C4
INDUSTRIAL ESTATES:		Orion Way. LU7	37 H3
Chartwell Business Pk. LU7	37 F6	Page's Ind Est. LU7	37 F5
Cherrycourt Way Ind Est. LU7	37 H4	Peartree La. LU7	37 E3
Chiltern Trading Est. LU7	37 E5	Pegasus Rd. LU7	37 G3
Greaves Way Ind Est. LU7	37 G5	Penley Way. LU7	37 E5
Grovebury Rd Ind Est. LU7	37 E5	Pennivale Clo. LU7	37 E2
Harmill Ind Est. LU7	37 E6	Phoenix Clo. LU7	37 H2
Page's Ind Est. LU7	37 F5	Plantation Rd. LU7	37 E1
Youngs Ind Est. LU7	37 H4	Plum Tree La. LU7	37 E3
Judges La. LU7	36 D4	Plummer Haven. LU7	37 E1
Jupiter Dri. LU7	37 H3	Poplar Clo. LU7	37 E1
Kendal Gdns. LU7	36 B4	Princess Ct. LU7	37 E3
Kennedy Ct. LU7	37 E3	Queen St. LU7	37 E3
Ketleys Grn. LU7	37 G3	Rannock Gdns. LU7	36 A3
King St. LU7	37 E2	Regent St. LU7	37 F3
Knaves Hill. LU7	36 B3	Richmond Rd. LU7	37 G5
Lake St. LU7	37 E4	Riverside. LU7	37 E2
Lammas Walk. LU7	37 E3	Rochester Mews. LU7	36 C4
*Lamsey Ct, Edward St. LU7	37 E3	Rock Clo. LU7	36 B4
Ledburn Gro. LU7	36 C5	Rock La. LU7	36 B4
Leedon Furlong. LU7	37 G3	Rockleigh Ct. LU7	36 C4
Leighton Rd. LU7	36 D4	Roosevelt Av. LU7	37 F2
Leighton Rd. LU7	37 H3	Rosebery Av. LU7	36 C3
Leopold Rd. LU7	36 C3	Rosebury Ct. LU7	36 D3
Leston Rd. LU7	37 E3	Rothschild Rd. LU7	36 D2
Leven Clo. LU7	36 A4	Rowley Furrows. LU7	36 C2
Lime Gro. LU7	36 D3	Russell Way. LU7	37 G4
Lincombe Slade. LU7	36 C2	Rye Clo. LU7	37 H3
Linwood Gro. LU7	37 F4	St Andrews Clo. LU7	37 E3
Lochy Dri. LU7	36 A3	St Andrews St. LU7	37 E3
Lomond Dri. LU7	36 A3	St Georges Clo. LU7	37 F3
Lovent Dri. LU7	37 F4	St Georges Ct. LU7	37 F2
Loyne Clo. LU7	36 A3	St Marys Clo. LU7	36 C3
Lyra Gdns. LU7	37 H3	St Marys Way. LU7	36 C3
Lywood Rd. LU7	37 G5	Sand Hills. LU7	37 F2
Malvern Dri. LU7	36 A2	Saturn Clo. LU7	37 H2
Mardle Rd. LU7	36 D5	Saxons Clo. LU7	37 G3
Maree Clo. LU7	36 A3	Shepherds Mead. LU7	37 E1
Market Sq. LU7	37 E4	Ship Rd. LU7	36 C4
Marley Fields. LU7	37 G4	Soulbury Rd. LU7	36 A2
		South St. LU7	37 F4
		Southcott Village. LU7	36 B5
		Southcourt Av. LU7	36 B4
		Southcourt Rd. LU7	36 C4
		Spencer Ct. LU7	37 F1
		Spring Side. LU7	36 C3
		Springfield Ct. LU7	36 C3
		Springfield Rd. LU7	36 C4

Stanbridge Rd. LU7	37 F4	Almond Clo. MK16	9 C3
Stanbridge Rd Ter. LU7	37 F4	Alston Dri. MK13	17 F2
Station App. LU7	36 C4	Althorpe Cres. MK13	13 E5
Station Rd. LU7	36 C3	Alton Gate. MK4	27 E5
Stephenson Clo. LU7	36 C4	Alverton. MK14	14 A3
Steppingstone Pl. LU7	37 F4	Ambergate. MK10	21 E3
Stoke Rd. LU7	36 B1	Ambridge Gro. MK6	23 H1
Stratton Mews. LU7	37 F4	Ambrose Ct. MK15	20 A5
Summer St. LU7	37 F3	Amherst St. MK15	14 D4
Talbot Ct. LU7	37 E2	Amos Ct. MK13	12 D5
The Chilterns. LU7	37 G5	Ampleforth. MK10	21 E6
The Elms. LU7	36 D4	Ancell Rd. MK11	10 D4
The Gables. LU7	36 C4	Andersen Gate. MK4	28 A6
The Maltings. LU7	37 F5	Andrewes Croft. MK14	14 A3
The Martins Dri. LU7	36 D2	Angel Clo. MK15	14 B4
The Paddocks. LU7	36 D3	Angelica Ct. MK7	25 E5
The Ride. LU7	37 H3	Anglesey Ct. MK8	17 G5
The Wood. LU7	37 E3	Angstrom Clo. MK5	22 B5
Threshers Ct. LU7	37 H3	Angus Dri. MK3	29 E2
Tiller Ct. LU7	37 H3	Annes Gro. MK14	13 G3
Tindall Av. LU7	37 F2	Annesley Rd. MK16	9 B3
Tree Walk. LU7	36 C2	Anson Rd. MK12	11 G3
Tudor Ct. LU7	36 D3	Anthony Ct. MK11	10 C4
Ullswater Dri. LU7	36 B4	Apple Croft. MK17	32 B4
Upper Coombe. LU7	36 C2	Appleby Heath. MK2	33 G2
Vandyke Rd. LU7	37 F3	Appleyard Pl. MK6	5 E6
Vicarage Gdns. LU7	36 C4	Arbroath Clo. MK8	29 E2
Vicarage Rd. LU7	36 C4	Arbrook Av. MK13	4 C2
Victoria Rd. LU7	36 C4	Archers Wells. MK3	29 G3
Vimy Rd. LU7	36 D4	Ardwell La. MK12	11 F4
Water La. LU7	36 D4	Arlington Gate. MK4	29 E2
Waterdell. LU7	37 G4	Arlott Cres. MK6	23 F2
Waterloo Rd. LU7	36 C4	Armourer Dri. MK14	19 F2
Wentworth Dri. LU7	37 E2	Armstrong Clo. MK8	26 E1
West St. LU7	36 D4	Arncliffe Dri. MK13	18 B3
Weston Av. LU7	37 G5	Arne La. MK7	25 G5
Westside. LU7	37 E3	Arrow Pl. MK2	33 H4
Wheatfield Clo. LU7	37 H3	Arundel Gro. MK3	29 E5
White Horse Ct. LU7	37 E3	Ascot Pl. MK3	32 B2
Willow Bank Walk. LU7	37 G2	Ash Hill Rd. MK16	9 B2
Windermere Gdns. LU7	36 A4	Ashburnham Clo. MK3	28 D4
Windsor Av. LU7	36 D3	Ashby. MK6	23 F2
Wing Rd. LU7	36 C5	Ashdown Clo. MK14	14 B3
Winston Clo. LU7	37 E2	Ashfield. MK14	13 F3
Woburn Pl. LU7	37 E1	Ashfield Gro. MK2	30 A5
Woodman Clo. LU7	37 F4	Ashpole Furlong. MK5	22 A3
Woodside Way. LU7	36 C5	Ashridge Clo. MK3	28 D5
Wyngates. LU7	36 C5	Ashwood. MK13	12 D4
Youngs Ind Est. LU7	37 H4	Astlethorpe. MK8	17 F4

MILTON KEYNES

		Aston Clo. MK5	22 B5
		Atherstone Ct. MK8	10 D3
Abbey Rd. MK13	17 G2	Atkins Clo. MK13	17 H2
Abbey Rd. MK16	24 C5	Atterbrook. MK13	17 G2
Abbey Ter. MK16	9 E2	Attingham Hill. MK8	17 G5
Abbey Way. MK13	13 E5	Atwell Clo. MK8	26 E1
Abbots Clo. MK13	13 E5	Auckland Pk. MK1	30 B1
Abbots Field. MK6	23 H2	Auden Clo. MK16	9 A1
Aberdeen Clo. MK3	29 E2	Audley Mead. MK13	17 H2
Abraham Clo. MK15	14 D5	Augustus Rd. MK11	10 C5
Ackroyd La. MK5	22 B5	Austwick La. MK4	28 B3
Acorn Walk. MK9	5 F3	Avebury Blvd. MK9	4 C6
Acton Gate. MK4	26 F4	Avington. MK8	17 F5
Adams Ct. MK6	24 A2	Avon Clo. MK16	9 E3
Adelphi St. MK9	19 F4	Avon Gro. MK3	28 D5
Ainsdale Clo. MK3	28 D4	Aylesbury St. MK2	30 C4
Aintree Clo. MK3	32 A2	Aylesbury St West.	
Akerman Clo. MK12	11 G4	MK12	11 G3
Albert St. MK2	30 A4	Aynho Ct. MK8	17 F5
Albion Pl. MK9	19 F5		
Albury Ct. MK8	17 F5	Baccara Gro. MK2	33 F2
Aldenham. MK6	24 B4	Back Leys. MK7	31 E2
Alder Mead. MK12	12 B6	Badgemore Ct. MK8	16 D3
Aldergill. MK13	18 C3	Badgers Oak. MK7	25 E3
Aldrich Dri. MK15	15 E4	Badminton Vw. MK8	17 G4
Aldwycks Clo. MK5	26 F1	Baily Ct. MK5	22 A5
Alexandra Dri. MK16	9 C4	Bala Clo. MK2	33 G3
All Saints Vw. MK5	22 B2	Bala Way. MK2	33 G3
Alladale Pl. MK12	17 E1	Balfe Mews. MK7	25 H6
Allen Clo. MK2	33 G3	Balmerino Clo. MK10	21 E6
Allerford Ct. MK5	22 C6	Balsam Clo. MK7	25 F4
Allison Ct. MK15	20 B6	Bampton Clo. MK4	28 D2
		Banburies Clo. MK4	29 F2
		Bank Top Pl. MK4	28 B2
		Bantock Clo. MK7	25 G5

Barbers Mews. MK14	19 F2	Birdlip La. MK7	25 E3
Barbury Ct. MK14	14 B3	Birkdale Clo. MK3	28 D5
Bardsey Ct. MK10	21 E6	Bishopstone. MK13	13 E6
Barford. MK11	11 E5	Blackberry Ct. MK7	25 F4
Barkers Croft. MK12	11 G5	Blackdown. MK11	11 E5
Barkestone Clo. MK4	28 C3	Blackham Clo. MK6	22 D3
Barleycroft. MK4	29 E1	Blackheath Cres. MK13	4 D1
Barnes Pl. MK6	22 D2	Blackhill Dri. MK12	11 F4
Barnfield Dri. MK6	24 A5	Blackmoor Gate. MK4	28 D3
Barnsbury Gdns. MK16	9 D3	Blackwell Pl. MK5	22 A6
Barnsdale Dri. MK4	27 E5	Blackwood Cres. MK13	12 C5
Barnstaple Ct. MK4	28 D2	Blakelands. MK14	9 A4
Barons Clo. MK2	30 A4	Blakelands Ind. Est.	
Barrett Pl. MK5	26 F1	MK14	14 B1
Barrington Mews. MK6	5 F6	Blakeney Ct. MK4	28 B5
Barry Av. MK13	13 F4	Blanchland Circle. MK10	25 E1
Bartholomew Clo. MK7	24 D5	Blandford Rd. MK13	13 E4
Barton Rd. MK2	33 F2	Blatherwick Ct. MK5	17 G6
Bascote. MK6	24 B5	Blaydon Clo. MK3	32 B2
Basildon Ct. MK8	17 G5	Bleak Hall Ind Est. MK6	23 E5
Baskerfield Gro. MK6	24 A2	Bleasdale. MK13	18 C2
Bassett Ct. MK16	9 D3	Blenheim Av. MK11	10 D5
Bates Clo. MK15	15 E4	Bletcham Way,	
Baxter Clo. MK8	26 E1	Caldecotte. MK7	30 D2
Bayard Av. MK14	19 E3	Bletcham Way. MK1	30 B3
Baynham Mead. MK7	25 E2	Bletcham Way. MK7	25 G5
Baytree Clo. MK17	32 B4	Bletchley Park Training	
Beacon Ct. MK4	28 D3	Centre. MK3	29 G4
Beaconsfield Pl. MK16	9 D2	Bletchley Rd. MK17	32 B4
Beadlemead. MK6	24 A4	Bletchley Rd. MK15	28 B1
Beales La. MK7	24 D5	Bliss Ct. MK7	25 F5
Beanfare. MK6	23 G6	Blisworth. MK6	24 B5
Beauchamp Clo. MK14	19 E1	Bluebell Croft. MK7	25 F4
Beaufort Dri. MK15	14 D4	Blundells Rd. MK13	13 E5
Beaumaris Gro. MK5	22 A4	Blythe Clo. MK16	9 E3
Beaverbrook Ct. MK3	29 F4	Bodiam Clo. MK5	22 A5
Bec La. MK15	14 C4	Bodle Clo. MK15	14 B5
Beckinsale Gro. MK8	17 E6	Bodnant Ct. MK4	27 F5
Bedford St. MK12	12 A5	Bolan Ct. MK8	26 E1
Bedford St. MK2	30 A5	Bolton Clo. MK3	29 F3
Bedgebury Pl. MK7	25 E1	Bomar Ct. MK1	29 H3
Beech Fern. MK7	25 E5	Bond Av. MK1	30 B3
Beech Rd. MK16	9 C3	Bonnards Rd. MK17	32 B4
Beechcroft Rd. MK3	32 C2	Booker Av. MK13	18 C4
Beethoven Clo. MK7	25 H6	Borodin Ct. MK7	25 G5
Beeward Clo. MK12	11 F4	Bossiney Pl. MK6	5 G5
Bekonscot Ct. MK14	14 B2	Bosworth Clo. MK3	29 E2
Bellini Clo. MK7	25 G5	Bottesford Clo. MK4	28 C3
Bellis Gro. MK6	24 A2	Boulters Lock. MK14	14 A1
Bells Mdw. MK15	14 C5	Boundary Cres. MK11	10 D3
Dellwether. MK11	11 F5	Bounds Croft. MK12	11 G5
Belmont Ct. MK8	16 D4	Bounty St. MK13	12 C4
Belsize Av. MK6	19 G6	Bourton Low. MK7	25 F5
Belvedere La. MK2	30 D4	Bowen Clo. MK7	25 G5
Belvoir Av. MK4	28 B4	Bowes Clo. MK16	9 D3
Benbow Ct. MK5	22 A3	Bowland Dri. MK4	28 B3
Bennet Clo. MK11	10 D5	Bowles Pl. MK6	24 B3
Bens Clo. MK19	8 C2	Bowling Leys. MK10	21 E5
Bentall Clo. MK15	14 D4	Bowood Ct. MK8	17 G5
Benwell Clo. MK13	17 G1	Bowyers Mews. MK14	19 E2
Berberis Clo. MK7	25 E5	Boxberry Gdns. MK7	25 E4
Bercham. MK8	17 F3	Boyce Cres. MK7	25 H5
Beretun. MK8	17 E4	Boycott Av. MK6	5 E6
Berevilles La. MK10	20 C5	Bradbourne Dri. MK7	31 F1
Bergamot Gdns. MK7	25 F5	Bradbury Clo. MK13	17 H2
Berkshire Grn. MK4	26 F4	Bradley Gro. MK4	28 B3
Berling Rd. MK8	17 F3	Bradvue Cres. MK13	13 E5
Bernay Gdns. MK15	14 C4	Bradwell Common Blvd.	
Bernstein Clo. MK7	25 G6	MK13	4 B3
Berrystead. MK7	31 E2	Bradwell Rd. MK13	12 D4
Berwald Clo. MK7	25 G6	Bradwell Rd,	
Berwick Dri. MK3	29 E3	Great Holm. MK5	17 H4
Bessemer Ct. MK14	14 B2	Bradwell Rd,	
Bettina Gro. MK2	33 F1	Loughton. MK5	22 A3
Bettys Clo. MK17	32 A5	Braford Gdns. MK5	22 B6
Beverley Pl. MK6	19 H6	Brahms Clo. MK7	25 G5
Bickleigh Cres. MK4	28 C1	Bramber Clo. MK3	29 E6
Bignell Croft. MK5	4 A5	Bramble Av. MK14	19 E3
Bilbrook La. MK4	22 C6	Bramley Rd. MK1	30 A2
Billingwell Pl. MK6	19 H5	Brampton Ct. MK13	12 D5
Bilton Rd. MK1	30 B3	Bransgill Ct. MK13	18 B3
Bingham Clo. MK4	28 B4	Bransworth Av. MK4	25 G2
Birchen Lee. MK4	28 C3	Brantham Clo. MK7	31 E2
Birchfield Gro. MK2	30 A5	Braunston. MK6	24 B4

Braybrooke Dri. MK4	29 E1	Burholme. MK4	28 C2
Brayton Ct. MK5	22 C4	Burners La. MK11	16 C2
Breamore Ct. MK8	17 F5	Burners La Sth. MK11	16 C2
Brearley Av. MK6	23 E2	Burnet. MK14	13 F4
Breckland. MK13	18 C2	Burnham Dri. MK13	4 B1
Bremen Gro. MK5	22 A6	Burnmoor Clo. MK2	33 G4
Brendon Ct. MK4	28 D2	Burns Clo. MK16	9 B2
Brent. MK6	24 B5	Burns Rd. MK3	33 E1
Bretby Chase. MK4	27 E5	Burtree Clo. MK12	12 B6
Breton. MK11	10 D3	Bury Av. MK16	9 D2
Briar Hill. MK12	17 E1	Bury Clo. MK16	9 D2
Briary View. MK17	27 B7	Bury St. MK16	9 D2
Brices Mdw. MK5	28 A2	Buscot Pl. MK8	17 G5
Brick Clo. MK11	16 C3	Bushey Bartrams. MK5	28 A2
Brickhill St. MK7	24 D2	Bushy Clo. MK3	29 F2
Brickhill St. MK14	14 B1	Butchers La. MK4	27 E5
Brickhill St,		Bute Brae. MK3	29 E2
Willen. MK15	14 C3	Butlers Gro. MK14	13 G3
Brickhill St,		Butterfield Clo. MK15	20 A6
Newlands. MK15	20 A3	Buttermere Clo. MK2	33 G2
Bridge Rd. MK19	8 B5	Buttermere Pl. MK2	33 G2
Bridge St. MK16	12 D4	Buzzacott La. MK4	28 C2
Bridgeford Ct. MK6	23 E2	Byerly Pl. MK14	19 F2
Bridgeturn Av. MK12	12 A3	Byrd Cres. MK7	25 G4
Bridgeway. MK13	12 D4	Byron Clo. MK3	32 D1
Bridle Clo. MK13	13 E5	Byron Dri. MK16	9 B2
Bridlington Cres. MK10	24 D1	Byward Clo. MK14	19 E1
Brill Pl. MK13	4 A2		
Brindlebrook. MK8	17 F4	Cadman Sq. MK5	22 C5
Brinklow Ind Est. MK7	25 F2	Caernarvon Cres. MK3	28 D6
Bristow Clo. MK2	30 C4	Caesars Clo. MK13	12 D6
Britten Gro. MK7	25 G5	Cairngorm Gate. MK6	22 D3
Broad Dean. MK6	23 G2	Caithness Ct. MK3	29 E2
Broad Piece. MK15	14 B4	Calamus Ct. MK7	25 E4
Broad St. MK16	9 C3	Caldecote Clo. MK16	15 F1
Broadarrow Clo. MK14	19 E1	Caldecote St. MK16	9 D3
Broadlands. MK6	23 H4	Caldecotte La. MK7	31 E1
Broadwater. MK6	24 B4	Caldecotte Lake Dri. MK7	31 E2
Broadway Av. MK14	14 A1	Caldewell. MK8	17 E4
Brockhampton. MK15	19 G2	Caledonian Rd. MK13	12 C4
Brockwell. MK16	9 D3	Calewen. MK8	17 F4
Bromham Mill. MK14	14 A1	Calluna Dri. MK3	29 F2
Brooke Clo. MK3	29 F5	Calvards Croft. MK12	11 G5
Brookfield Rd. MK19	12 A1	Calverleigh Cres. MK4	28 C2
Brookfield Rd. MK17	32 B5	Calverton La. MK19	16 B5
Brooklands Rd. MK2	30 A5	Calverton Rd. MK11	10 C4
Brookside. MK12	17 E1	Calves Clo. MK5	28 A1
Brookside Clo. MK19	10 A3	Cam Ct. MK3	28 D5
Broomfield. MK12	17 E1	Camber Clo. MK3	28 D6
Broomlee. MK13	12 D6	Cambridge St. MK12	11 H3
Brora Clo. MK2	33 G3	Cambridge St. MK2	30 A4
Brough Clo. MK5	22 A5	Cambron. MK8	17 E4
Broughton Grounds La.		Camlet Gro. MK14	13 G4
MK17	21 F3	Camomile Ct. MK7	25 F5
Broughton Rd. MK10	20 D5	Campania Clo. MK10	21 E5
Brownbaker Ct. MK14	19 F2	Campion. MK14	14 A1
Browne Willis Clo. MK2	30 B5	Candlewicks. MK7	25 F4
Browning Clo. MK16	9 B2	Canons Rd. MK12	11 G2
Browning Cres. MK3	33 E1	Cantle Av. MK14	19 F3
Broxbourne Clo. MK14	14 B1	Capel Dri. MK14	19 F2
Bruckner Gdns. MK7	25 G5	Capital Dri. MK14	18 D1
Brudenell Dri. MK7	25 F2	Capron. MK6	23 G5
Brunleys. MK11	16 C3	Caraway Clo. MK7	25 E6
Brushford Clo. MK4	28 D2	Cardigan Clo. MK3	29 F4
Bryony Pl. MK14	19 E3	Cardwell Clo. MK4	28 C3
Buckby. MK6	24 B4	Carenter Ct. MK14	19 F1
Buckfast Av. MK3	29 F3	Carhampton Ct. MK4	28 D2
Buckingham Ct. MK16	9 C3	Carleton Gate. MK15	15 F4
Buckingham Gate. MK6	23 G1	Carlina Pl. MK14	5 E1
Buckingham Rd. MK3	29 E6	Carlton Clo. MK16	9 F2
Buckingham St. MK12	12 A5	Carlyle Clo. MK16	9 A2
Buckland Dri. MK6	23 H4	Carnot Clo. MK5	22 C6
Buckman Clo. MK12	11 G4	Carnoustie Gro. MK3	28 C6
Buckthorn. MK12	12 C6	Carolus Creek. MK15	14 C4
Bull La. MK2	30 B4	Carrick Rd. MK6	5 G5
Bullington End Rd. MK19	8 C2	Carrington Rd. MK16	9 C3
Bunsty Ct. MK11	11 E5	Carroll Clo. MK16	9 B1
Burano Gro. MK7	25 G4	Carteret Clo. MK15	15 F4
Burchard Cres. MK5	22 A3	Carters La. MK11	16 B2
Burdeleys La. MK5	22 A6	Cartmel Clo. MK3	32 A2
Burdock Ct. MK16	9 A2	Cartwright Pl. MK6	22 D2
Burewelle. MK8	17 E4	Carvers Mews. MK14	19 E2
Burgess Gdns. MK16	9 C4	Cashmere Clo. MK5	22 A6
Burghley Ct. MK8	17 F5	Casterton Clo. MK13	18 C3

Castle Meadow Clo. MK16	9 E2	Church End Rd. MK5	28 A1
Castle Rose. MK6	24 B3	Church Farm Cres. MK14	13 H3
Castlesteads. MK13	17 G1	Church Green Rd. MK3	29 E5
Catchpole Clo. MK12	11 F4	Church Hill. MK8	17 F4
Cathay Clo. MK3	33 E1	Church La. MK17	27 B6
Cavendish Ct. MK5	17 G6	Church La. MK5	22 B2
Cavenham. MK8	17 F3	Church Lees. MK14	13 G2
Cawardon. MK14	13 F4	Church Rd. MK17	31 G3
Caxton Rd. MK12	11 G2	Church St. MK11	10 C4
Cecily Ct. MK5	22 A5	Church St. MK12	12 A4
Cedar Lodge Dri. MK12	12 B4	Church St. MK13	12 D4
Cedars Way. MK16	9 D2	Church St. MK2	30 C4
Celandine Ct. MK7	25 E4	Church Vw. MK16	9 E2
Celina Clo. MK2	33 G2	Church Walk. MK3	29 E5
Century Av. MK6	22 D3	Cinnamon Gro. MK7	25 E5
Chadds La. MK6	23 H2	City Sq. MK9	5 E3
Chadwick Dri. MK6	23 H3	Civic Walk. MK9	5 E3
Chaffron Way. MK10	20 D6	Clailey Ct. MK11	11 E4
Chaffron Way. MK15	20 A6	Clapham Pl. MK13	4 B3
Chaffron Way,		Claremont Av. MK11	10 D5
Emerson Valley. MK5	28 A3	Clarence Rd. MK11	10 D4
Chaffron Way,		Clarendon Dri. MK8	17 F3
Shenley Lodge. MK5	22 C6	Claridge Dri. MK10	21 E6
Chaffron Way. MK6	23 E3	Clarke Rd. MK1	30 A1
Chalcot Pl. MK8	17 F5	Clay Hill. MK8	17 E3
Chalfont Clo. MK13	12 D5	Clayton Gate. MK14	14 B3
Chalkdell Dri. MK4	26 F3	Cleavers Av. MK14	4 D1
Challacombe. MK4	28 D3	Cleeve Cres. MK3	29 F3
Chalmers Av. MK19	12 A1	Clegg Sq. MK5	22 B5
Chalwell Ridge. MK5	28 B1	Clerkenwell Pl. MK6	19 G5
Champflower. MK4	28 C1	Cleveland. MK13	13 E5
Chancery Clo. MK13	12 D5	Clifford Av. MK2	30 A5
Chandlers Ct. MK6	24 C5	Cline Ct. MK8	26 E1
Chaplin Gro. MK8	26 D1	Cloebury Paddock.	
Chapman Av. MK14	19 F2	MK15	20 A4
Chapter. MK6	23 F5	Cloudberry. MK7	25 E4
Charbray Cres. MK5	22 A6	Cloutsham Clo. MK4	28 C2
Chardacre. MK8	17 E4	Clover Clo. MK5	22 A2
Charles Way. MK16	9 D2	Clovers La. MK13	18 B3
Charlock Ct. MK6	9 A2	Cluny Ct. MK7	25 G4
Chart Ley Ct. MK5	28 B1	Clydesdale Pl. MK14	19 E3
Chartwell Rd. MK16	9 F3	Coachmaker Ct. MK14	19 F2
Chase Av. MK7	25 E6	Cobb Hall Rd. MK17	32 A5
Chatsworth. MK8	17 F5	Coberley Clo. MK15	19 G2
Chaucer Clo. MK16	9 B3	Cockerell Gro. MK5	22 B5
Chaucer Rd. MK3	33 E1	Coddimoor La. MK17	27 B8
Chawton Cres. MK8	17 G4	Cofferidge Clo. MK11	10 C4
Cheltenham Gdns. MK3	32 B2	Cogan Ct. MK8	26 E1
Cheneys Walk. MK3	29 G2	Coggeshall Gro. MK7	25 G3
Chepstow Dri. MK3	32 A2	Coldeaton. MK4	28 B2
Cheriton. MK8	28 D1	Coleridge Clo. MK16	9 A2
Cherleton. MK8	17 E4	Coleridge Clo. MK3	33 E1
Cherry Rd. MK16	9 C3	Colesbourne Dri. MK15	19 G1
Chervil. MK6	23 G5	Coleshill Pl. MK13	4 B1
Chesham Av. MK13	4 B1	Colley Hill. MK13	17 G1
Cheslyn Gdns. MK14	14 B3	Colne. MK6	24 B4
Chesney Wold. MK6	23 E4	Colston Basset. MK4	28 B4
Chester Clo. MK3	28 D6	Colts Holm Rd. MK12	11 G1
Chesterholm. MK13	12 D6	Coltsfoot Pl. MK14	4 D1
Chestnut Clo. MK11	10 C4	Columbia Pl. MK9	19 F5
Chestnut Clo. MK17	32 A6	Combe Martin. MK4	28 C2
Chestnut Cres. MK2	30 B6	Comfrey Clo. MK7	25 E5
Chetwode Av. MK10	25 E1	Common La. MK13	17 H1
Chevalier Dri. MK8	17 E6	Common La. MK5	22 C2
Chicheley St. MK16	9 F2	Condor Clo. MK6	23 G2
Chicksands Av. MK10	21 E6	Congreve. MK6	24 B5
Chieveley Ct. MK4	28 C3	Coniston Way. MK2	33 G2
Childs Way. MK5	22 A6	Conniburrow Blvd. MK14	18 D4
Childs Way. MK9	4 D6	Constable Clo. MK14	19 E1
Chillery Leys. MK15	15 F4	Constantine Way. MK13	12 C6
Chingle Croft. MK4	28 B3	Conway Cres. MK3	29 E5
Chippenham Dri. MK10	21 F6	Cook Clo. MK7	25 E6
Chipperfield Clo. MK13	12 D4	Coopers Mews. MK14	19 E1
Chipping Vale. MK4	28 B3	Copeland Clo. MK5	25 G5
Chirbury Gate. MK10	25 E1	Copes Haven. MK5	28 B1
Chislehampton. MK15	20 A4	Coppin La. MK13	17 H2
Chiswick Clo. MK4	27 F5	Corbett Clo. MK15	15 E4
Christian Ct. MK15	15 E4	Cordwainer Ct. MK14	19 F1
Christie Clo. MK16	9 A1	Corfe Cres. MK3	29 E4
Church Clo. MK5	22 B2	Coriander Ct. MK7	25 F5
Church End, Newton		Corin Clo. MK2	33 G3
Longville. MK17	32 B4	Corn Hill. MK8	17 E4
Church End,		Cornbury Cres. MK15	19 G2
Wavendon. MK17	25 H3	Cornelia Clo. MK2	33 G2

Name	Ref
Cornwall Gro. MK3	29 E4
Coronation Rd. MK11	10 D5
Corrigan Clo. MK3	29 F5
Corsham Ct. MK8	17 G5
Cosgrove Rd. MK19	10 B2
Cotman Clo. MK12	11 G4
Cottage Common. MK5	4 A6
Cottesloe Ct. MK11	11 E4
Cottingham Gro. MK3	33 E1
Cottisford Cres. MK14	14 A2
Countisbury. MK4	28 D2
Coverack Pl. MK4	28 B5
Coverdale. MK13	18 B2
Cowdray Clo. MK15	20 A4
Cowper Clo. MK16	9 B2
Craddocks Clo. MK13	17 H2
Craigmore Av. MK3	29 E5
Cranberry Clo. MK7	25 E4
Cranborne Av. MK4	27 E5
Cranborne Cres. MK4	27 E5
Crane Ct.. MK5	4 A5
Cranesbill Pl. MK14	18 D4
Cranwell Clo. MK5	28 B2
Creed St. MK12	12 B4
Creslow Ct. MK11	11 E4
Cressey Av. MK5	28 B1
Cricklebeck. MK13	18 B3
Crispin Rd. MK13	13 E4
Crofts La. MK17	32 B5
Cromarty Ct. MK3	29 E2
Crompton Rise. MK4	28 A3
Cromwell Av. MK16	9 A3
Cropwell Bishop. MK4	28 B4
Crosby Ct. MK8	26 E1
Cross St. MK16	9 D2
Crosshills. MK11	10 C5
Crosslands. MK14	13 G3
Crowborough La. MK7	25 E2
Crown Walk. MK9	5 F2
Crownhill Ind Est. MK8	17 F6
Crowther Ct. MK5	22 C5
Croydon Clo. MK4	28 C1
Cruickshank Gro. MK8	17 E6
Crummock Pl. MK2	33 G2
Culbertson La. MK13	12 C5
Cullen Pl. MK2	33 G3
Culmstock Clo. MK4	28 D3
Culrain Pl. MK12	16 D1
Culross Gro. MK10	21 E6
Cumbria Clo. MK3	29 E4
Currier Dri. MK14	19 E1
Curtis Croft. MK5	28 B1
Curzon Pl. MK7	25 H6
Cutlers Mews. MK14	19 E2
Cypress. MK16	9 B3
Dalton Gate. MK10	20 D4
Dalvina Pl. MK12	16 D1
Dane Rd. MK1	30 B3
Daniels Welch. MK6	23 F3
Dansteed Way. MK13	18 A6
Dansteed Way. MK14	18 D3
Dansteed Way, Willen. MK15	14 D4
Dansteed Way, Pennyland. MK15	19 F1
Dansteed Way. MK8	17 F5
Darby Clo. MK5	22 B5
Darin Ct. MK8	17 F6
Darley Gate. MK14	19 F3
Darnel Clo. MK6	23 G5
Dart Clo. MK16	9 E3
Daubeney Gate. MK5	26 F1
Davenport Lea. MK7	25 H5
Davy Av. MK5	22 C3
Dawson Rd. MK1	30 A1
Daylesford Ct. MK15	19 G2
Deans Rd. MK12	11 G2
Deanshanger Rd. MK19	10 A4
Debbs Clo. MK11	10 D3
Deben Clo. MK16	9 E3
Deepdale. MK13	18 C2
Deer Walk. MK9	5 F2
Deerfern Clo. MK14	13 H2
Delaware Dri. MK15	14 D3
Delius Clo. MK7	25 F5
Deltic Av. MK13	18 B5
Denbigh East Ind Est. MK1	30 B3
Denbigh Hall Dri. MK3	29 E1
Denbigh Hall Ind Est. MK3	29 F1
Denbigh Rd. MK1	29 G2
Denbigh Way. MK2	30 A4
Denbigh West Ind Est. MK1	29 G3
Denchworth Ct. MK4	28 B3
Denesbrook Clo. MK4	22 D6
Denham Clo. MK3	28 C4
Denison Ct. MK7	25 G4
Denmark St. MK2	30 B4
Denmead. MK8	17 F3
Dere Pl. MK2	33 H4
Derwent Clo. MK16	9 E3
Derwent Dri. MK3	29 E4
Develin Clo. MK14	19 E1
Devon Clo. MK3	29 E4
Dexter Av. MK6	5 G6
Dickens Dri. MK19	10 A3
Dickens Rd. MK12	11 H1
Diddington Clo. MK2	33 G5
Dixie La. MK7	25 G4
Dodkin. MK6	23 H5
Dodman Grn. MK4	28 B5
Dolben Ct. MK15	15 E3
Donnington. MK13	13 E5
Doon Way. MK2	33 F3
Dorchester Av. MK3	29 F2
Doreen Clo. MK4	33 F1
Dorking Pl. MK5	28 B1
Dormans Clo. MK10	20 D5
Dorney Pl. MK13	4 B2
Dorset Clo. MK3	29 E4
Dorton Clo. MK8	17 F4
Douglas Pl. MK6	22 D2
Dove Clo. MK16	9 E3
Dovecote. MK16	9 C2
Dovecote Croft. MK14	13 H2
Dover Gate. MK3	29 E5
Down Dean. MK6	23 G2
Downland. MK8	17 F3
Downley Av. MK13	4 C1
Downs Barn Blvd. MK14	19 E3
Downs Vw. MK17	31 G3
Drakes Mews. MK8	17 F5
Drakewell Rd. MK17	31 H3
Drayton Rd, Newton Longville. MK17	32 A6
Drayton Rd, Water Eaton. MK17	33 E6
Drayton Rd. MK2	33 G2
Drovers Croft. MK12	11 G5
Drummound Hay. MK15	14 D5
Dryden Clo. MK16	9 B3
Duchess Gro. MK7	25 F3
Dudley Hill. MK5	22 A4
Dukes Dri. MK2	30 A4
Dulverton Dri. MK4	28 C2
Dulwich Clo. MK16	9 C4
Dumfries Clo. MK3	29 F2
Dunbar Clo. MK3	28 C4
Duncan Gro. MK5	26 F2
Dunchurch Dale. MK7	25 E5
Duncombe St. MK2	30 A5
Dunkery Beacon. MK4	28 C2
Dunsby Rd. MK6	23 F6
Dunster Clo. MK4	28 D2
Dunvedin Pl. MK12	17 E2
Dunvegan Clo. MK2	33 G4
Duparc Clo. MK7	25 G5
Durgate. MK7	24 D2
Durrans Clo. MK2	30 C4
Dyers Mews. MK14	19 E2
Dyersdale. MK13	18 C2
Eagle Walk. MK9	5 F2
Earls Clo. MK2	30 A4
Earls Willow. MK13	12 D4
East Chapel. MK4	28 B5
East Dales. MK13	18 C2
East La. MK7	24 D3
Eastbury Ct. MK4	28 C3
Eaton Av. MK2	30 B5
Ebbsgrove. MK5	4 A5
Eddington Ct. MK4	28 C3
Eden Walk. MK3	28 D4
Edgecote. MK8	17 G5
Edison Sq. MK5	22 B5
Edmund Ct. MK5	26 F1
Edrich Av. MK6	23 E2
Edwin Clo. MK17	31 G3
Edy Ct. MK5	17 H5
Egerton Gate. MK5	22 A6
Egmont Av. MK11	10 D5
Elder Gate. MK9	4 A4
Elfords. MK6	23 F4
Elgar Gro. MK7	25 F5
Eliot Clo. MK16	9 A1
Ellbrook Av. MK13	4 B3
Ellenstow. MK13	17 G1
Ellerburn Pl. MK4	28 B2
Ellesborough Gro. MK8	17 E3
Ellisgill Ct. MK13	18 B3
Elm Clo. MK17	32 A6
Elmers Pk. MK3	29 F5
Elmhurst Clo. MK4	29 E1
Elmridge Ct. MK4	28 C3
Elthorne Way. MK16	9 C4
Elton. MK6	24 B3
Emerton Gdns. MK11	10 D4
Emmett Clo. MK4	28 B3
Empingham Clo. MK2	33 G4
Enfield Chase. MK1	18 C3
Engaine Dri. MK5	26 F1
Enmore Gate. MK6	19 G5
Ennell Gro. MK2	33 G3
Ennerdale Clo. MK2	33 H3
Enterprise La. MK9	19 G5
Epsom Gro. MK3	32 B2
Erica Rd. MK12	17 F1
Eridge Grn. MK7	25 E2
Eskan Ct. MK9	19 G3
Essenden Ct. MK11	11 E4
Essex Clo. MK3	29 F3
Eston Ct. MK13	12 D5
Etheridge Av. MK7	25 F2
Ethorpe. MK8	17 F4
Eton Cres. MK12	11 G3
Evans Gate. MK6	5 E6
Evelyn Pl. MK13	12 D4
Everglade. MK6	23 G2
Everley Clo. MK4	28 B2
Exbridge. MK4	28 C1
Exmoor Ct. MK4	28 D2
*Eynsham Ct, Pattison La. MK15	20 A6
Fadmoor Pl. MK4	28 B2
Fairfax. MK13	13 F5
Fairford Cres. MK15	19 G2
Fairways. MK8	16 D3
Falaise Nook. MK15	14 C4
Falcon Av. MK6	19 G5
Falmourth Pl. MK6	5 G5
Faraday Dri. MK5	22 C5
Farinton. MK8	17 F4
Farjeon Ct. MK7	25 H5
Farmborough. MK6	24 A4
Farnham Ct. MK8	17 F5
Farrier Pl. MK14	19 F2
Farthing Gro. MK6	23 H4
Favell Dri. MK4	29 E1
Featherstone Rd. MK12	11 F4
Fegans Ct. MK11	10 C3
Felbridge. MK7	25 E3
Fennel Dri. MK14	18 D3
Fenny Lock Ind Est. MK1	30 C3
Fennymere. MK8	17 E4
Fenton Ct. MK8	17 G5
Fern Gro. MK2	33 G3
Fernan Dell. MK8	17 E6
Fernborough Haven. MK4	28 C3
Ferndale. MK6	23 G1
Field La. MK12	11 G4
Field Walk. MK9	5 G2
Finch Clo. MK10	20 D4
Findlay Way. MK2	30 A5
Fingle Dri. MK13	12 C4
Fire La. MK17	32 B4
First Av. MK1	29 H3
Fishermead Blvd. MK6	5 G5
Fitzhamon Ct. MK12	11 F4
Flambard Clo. MK15	14 B4
Flaxbourne Ct. MK7	25 G3
Flaxley Gate. MK10	21 E6
Fleming Dri. MK6	23 G4
Fletchers Mews. MK14	19 E2
Flintergill Ct. MK13	18 B3
Flitton Ct. MK11	11 E5
Flora Thompson Dri. MK16	9 A1
Florin Clo. MK15	14 B4
Fontwell Dri. MK3	32 A3
Forches Clo. MK4	28 C3
Fordcombe Lea. MK7	25 E2
Forest Rise. MK6	23 G2
Forfar Dri. MK3	29 E3
Formby Clo. MK3	28 C6
Forrabury Av. MK13	4 B2
Fortescue Dri. MK5	22 A4
Fortuna Ct. MK7	25 G4
Fosters La. MK13	17 H3
Founders Mews. MK14	19 F1
Fountaine Clo. MK14	13 H4
Fowler. MK14	13 F4
Fox Gate. MK16	9 C2
Fox Milne Ind Est. MK15	20 C3
Foxcovert Rd. MK4	26 F3
Foxglove Ct. MK16	9 A2
Foxhunter Dri. MK14	18 D1
Foxton. MK6	24 B4
Framlingham Ct. MK5	22 A5
France Furlong. MK14	14 A3
Francis Ct. MK5	22 A4
Frank Atter Croft. MK12	11 H4
Franklins Croft. MK12	12 A6
Freeman Clo. MK12	11 G4
Frensham Dri. MK2	33 F1
Friary Gdns. MK16	9 D4
Frithwood Cres. MK7	25 E3
Froxfield Ct. MK4	28 C3
Fryday St. MK6	23 E3
Fulmer St. MK4	28 B1
Fulmer St. MK5	26 F1
Fulmer St. MK8	26 D1
Fulwoods Dri. MK6	23 F2
Furness Cres. MK3	29 F3
Fury Ct. MK8	26 E1
Furze Way. MK12	11 H3
Fyfield Barrow. MK7	25 F4
Gable Thorne. MK7	25 G4
Gabriel Clo. MK7	25 G5
Gaddesden Cres. MK7	25 F4
Gairloch Clo. MK2	33 H3
Gallagher Clo. MK8	17 E6
Galley Hill. MK11	11 E4
Galloway Clo. MK3	29 E2
Ganton Clo. MK3	28 D4
Garamonde Dri. MK8	17 F3
Garbo Clo. MK8	17 E6
Gardiner Ct. MK13	12 C5
Garland Ct. MK8	17 E6
Garraways. MK6	23 F3
Garret Dri. MK13	17 H3
Garron Ct. MK2	33 G4
Garrowmore Gro. MK2	33 H3
Garry Clo. MK2	33 F3
Garston. MK8	17 F4
Garthwaite Cres. MK5	22 A4
Gaskin Ct. MK14	19 F2
Gatcombe. MK8	17 F4
Gatewick La. MK7	31 E2
Gayal Croft. MK5	28 B1
George St. MK2	30 C4
Germander Pl. MK14	18 D3

Gershwin Ct. MK7	25 G6
Gibbwin. MK14	13 G3
Gibsons Grn. MK13	18 B4
Gifford Gate. MK14	13 H4
Gilbert Clo. MK3	33 E1
Gisburn Clo. MK13	18 B3
Gladstone Clo. MK16	9 D4
Glamorgan Clo. MK3	29 E3
Glastonbury Clo. MK3	29 F3
Glazier Dri. MK14	19 E2
Glebe Clo. MK5	17 G6
Gledfield Pl. MK12	17 E1
Gleeman Clo. MK12	11 F4
Gleneagles Clo. MK3	28 D5
Glenwoods. MK16	9 D3
Gliders Mews. MK14	19 E1
Gloucester Rd. MK12	12 A6
Glyn Sq. MK12	12 B4
Glyn St. MK13	12 D4
Goathland Croft. MK4	28 B2
Goddards Croft. MK12	11 H4
Godwin Clo. MK7	25 F3
Golden Dri. MK6	23 G3
Goldilocks. MK7	25 E4
Goldmark Clo. MK7	25 H5
Goldsmith Dri. MK16	9 A2
Golspie Croft. MK12	16 D1
Goodman Gdns. MK6	24 B2
Goodwick Gro. MK4	28 B5
Goodwood. MK8	17 F5
Goran Av. MK11	10 D5
Gordale. MK13	18 B2
Goring. MK14	13 F4
Gorman Pl. MK2	33 H4
Gorricks. MK11	10 C5
Goslington. MK1	29 H2
Goudhurst Ct. MK7	25 E3
Grace Av. MK6	22 D2
Grafham Clo. MK14	14 B3
Grafton Gate. MK9	4 B4
Grafton Park. MK9	4 C5
Grafton St. MK1	29 G1
Grafton St. MK13	12 B4
Grafton St. MK13	17 H1
Grafton St. MK6	22 D2
Grampian Gate. MK6	22 D3
Gramwell. MK5	26 F1
Granby St. MK1	29 G2
Granes End. MK14	14 A3
Grange Rd. MK3	29 F5
Grangers Croft. MK12	16 D1
Grantham Ct. MK5	22 C5
Grasmere Way. MK2	33 G2
Grass Croft. MK4	29 E1
Grassington. MK13	12 D6
Graveney Pl. MK6	19 G6
Great Chesters. MK13	12 D6
Great Denson. MK6	23 G2
Great Ground. MK14	13 H4
Great Linch. MK10	21 E5
Great Monks St. MK12	11 F3
Great Monks St. MK12	17 E1
Great Monks St. MK8	17 E2
Greatheed Dell. MK7	25 H6
Green Farm Rd. MK16	9 D3
Green La. MK12	12 A5
Green Park Dri. MK16	9 C4
Green Way. MK17	32 B4
Greenfield Rd. MK16	9 B3
Greenhill Clo. MK5	17 G6
Greenlands Clo. MK16	9 B3
Greenlaw Pl. MK3	29 F2
Greenleys La. MK12	11 G5
Greenside Hill. MK4	28 B4
Greenways. MK17	31 F3
Greenwich Gdns. MK16	9 C4
Gregories Dri. MK7	25 F3
Greystonley. MK4	28 C3
Greyfriars St. MK6	21 F6
Griffith Gate. MK10	21 E5
Griffon Clo. MK6	23 G2
Grimbald Ct. MK5	14 D4
Grizedale. MK13	18 B2
Groombridge. MK7	25 E3
Grosmont Clo. MK4	28 B2
Groundsell Clo. MK7	25 F4
Grove Ash. MK1	30 B1
Groves Brook. MK17	31 G3
Groveway. MK3	29 F1
Groveway, Beanhill. MK6	23 G6
Groveway, Netherfield. MK6	24 A5
Groveway. MK7	25 E4
Guest Gdns. MK13	13 E3
Gundale Ct. MK4	28 A2
Gunmaker Ct. MK14	19 F2
Gunver La. MK4	28 A4
Gurnards Av. MK6	5 H4
Gurney Clo. MK5	22 A3
Gwynant Ct. MK2	33 G5
Haberley Mead. MK13	17 H2
Haddington Clo. MK3	29 E2
Haddon. MK8	17 F5
Hadley Pl. MK13	4 C2
Hadrians Dri. MK13	12 D6
Hainault Av. MK14	14 B2
Haithwaite. MK8	17 E4
Haldene. MK8	17 F3
Hale Av. MK11	10 D4
Hall Clo. MK19	10 A3
Halswell Pl. MK10	21 E5
Halton Chesters. MK13	12 D5
Haly Clo. MK13	17 H2
Hambleton Gro. MK4	28 A3
Hamburg Croft. MK5	28 B1
Hamilton La. MK3	32 A2
Hamlins. MK6	23 F4
Hammerwood Gate. MK7	24 D3
Hammond Cres. MK15	14 C5
Hampshire Ct. MK3	29 F3
Hampson Clo. MK3	17 H1
Hampstead Gate. MK13	4 C2
Hampton. MK8	17 G5
Handel Mead. MK7	25 H5
Hanmer Rd. MK6	24 C5
Hanscomb Clo. MK15	20 A5
Hansen Croft. MK5	22 B5
Hanslope Rd. MK19	8 B1
Harborne Ct. MK8	16 D4
Harby Clo. MK4	28 B4
Harcourt. MK8	17 G2
Harding Rd. MK7	25 G2
Harebell Clo. MK7	25 F5
Hareden Croft. MK4	28 B3
Hargreaves Nook. MK14	14 C1
Harkness Clo. MK2	33 G2
Harlans Clo. MK6	23 G2
Harlech Pl. MK3	29 E5
Harlequin Pl. MK8	26 F4
Harlestone Ct. MK14	14 B2
Harnett Dri. MK12	11 E3
Harpers La. MK14	14 A3
Harrier Ct. MK6	23 G2
Harrier Dri. MK6	23 F2
Harrison Clo. MK5	22 D4
Harrowden. MK13	13 E4
Harthames. MK5	28 A2
Hartfield Clo. MK7	25 E2
Hartland Av. MK4	18 B4
Hartley. MK14	13 H3
Hartwort Clo. MK7	25 F4
Harvard Clo. MK14	14 A1
Harvester Clo. MK12	11 F4
Harwood St. MK13	12 D4
Hasgill Ct. MK13	18 B3
Haslow Ct. MK8	17 E3
Hastings. MK11	10 D4
Hatchlands. MK8	17 F4
Hathaway Ct. MK8	17 E6
Hatton. MK6	24 B4
Hauksbee Gdns. MK5	22 C5
Haversham Rd. MK19	12 B2
Hawkhurst Gate. MK7	24 D2
Hawkins Clo. MK11	10 C4
Hawkmoor Clo. MK6	23 H2
Hawkridge. MK4	29 E2
Hawkwell Est. MK19	10 A3
Hawthorn Av. MK2	30 C5
Haydock Clo. MK3	32 A2
Haynes Way. MK17	31 G3
Haythrop Clo. MK15	19 G1
Haywards Croft. MK12	11 G4
Hazel Gro. MK2	30 B6
Hazel Wood. MK14	14 A3
Hazelhurst. MK4	28 B3
Heaney Clo. MK16	9 B1
Hearne Pl. MK6	23 E2
Heather Croft. MK14	13 H4
Heathfield. MK12	17 E1
Heaton Clo. MK8	26 D1
Hedges Ct. MK5	22 B4
Hedingham Clo. MK5	22 A5
Hele Ct. MK7	31 E2
Helford Pl. MK6	23 G1
Helston Pl. MK6	5 H5
Hemingway Clo. MK16	9 A2
Henders. MK11	10 D4
Hendrix Dri. MK8	17 E6
Hengistbury La. MK4	27 F6
Hensman Gate. MK10	20 D4
Hepleswell. MK8	17 E4
Herdman Clo. MK12	11 G4
Herriot Clo. MK16	9 B2
Hertford Pl. MK3	29 E3
Hetton Clo. MK13	18 C4
Hexham Gdns. MK3	32 B2
Heybridge Cres. MK7	31 E2
Heydon Ct. MK13	12 D4
Higgs Ct. MK5	17 G5
High Halden. MK7	25 F2
High Park Dri. MK12	11 F3
High St. MK11	10 B3
High St. MK19	12 D1
High St. MK13	12 D4
High St. MK14	13 H2
High St. MK16	9 D2
High St. MK17	27 B6
High Trees. MK6	23 F2
Highfield Clo. MK16	9 F3
Highfield Clo. MK3	29 G3
Highgate Over. MK7	25 E3
Highgrove Hill. MK8	17 F5
Highland Clo. MK3	29 E2
Highveer Croft. MK4	28 B4
Hill View. MK16	9 B3
Hillcrest Clo. MK5	22 B4
Hilliard Dri. MK13	17 G2
Hills Clo. MK14	14 A4
Hillyer Ct. MK6	23 H1
Hindemith Gdns. MK7	25 G5
Hindhead Knoll. MK7	25 F4
Hinton Ct. MK3	29 F4
Hoathly Mews. MK7	25 E2
Hobart Cres. MK15	14 C5
Hockliffe Brae. MK7	25 F5
Hodder La. MK4	28 C2
Hodge Lea La. MK12	16 D1
Hodgemore Ct. MK14	14 B1
Hogarths Ct. MK8	17 G4
Holdom Av. MK1	30 B3
Holland Way. MK16	9 C3
Holliday Clo. MK8	26 E1
Hollin La. MK12	17 F1
Hollinwell Clo. MK3	28 C4
Holly Clo. MK8	26 E1
Holme Wood. MK4	29 E1
Holmfield Clo. MK6	24 B4
Holmgate. MK5	17 G5
Holst Cres. MK7	25 G6
Holt Gro. MK5	22 A2
Holton Hill. MK4	28 C3
Holy Thorn La. MK5	22 A5
Holyhead Cres. MK4	28 B5
Holyrood. MK8	17 F5
Holywell Pl. MK6	19 H5
Home Clo. MK3	29 G3
Home Farm. MK17	32 B4
Home Field. MK7	31 E1
Homestall Clo. MK5	17 G6
Homeward Ct. MK5	22 B3
Honeypot Clo. MK13	17 H2
Honiton Ct. MK7	25 G3
Hooper Gate. MK15	14 D4
Hopkins Clo. MK10	20 D5
Hoppers Mdw. MK5	17 G5
Horn La. MK11	10 C4
Hornbeam. MK16	9 B3
Hornby Chase. MK4	28 A3
Horners Croft. MK12	11 H4
Horsefair Grn. MK11	10 C4
Horton Gate. MK14	14 B1
Horwood Ct. MK1	30 B3
Houghton Ct. MK8	17 F5
Housman Clo. MK16	9 B1
Howe Rock Pl. MK4	28 B4
Hoylake Clo. MK3	28 C6
Huckleberry Clo. MK7	25 F4
Hudson La. MK8	17 E6
Humber Way. MK3	29 E4
Hunsdon Clo. MK14	13 G5
Hunstanton Way. MK3	28 D5
Hunter Dri. MK2	33 G2
Hunters Reach. MK13	17 H2
Huntingbrooke. MK8	17 G5
Huntingdon Cres. MK3	32 A2
Huntsman Gro. MK14	14 C1
Hurley Croft. MK10	21 E6
Hurlstone Gro. MK4	28 D2
Hutchings Clo. MK5	17 G5
Hutton Av. MK6	5 F6
Huxley Clo. MK16	9 A2
Hyde Clo. MK16	9 C4
Ibstone Av. MK13	18 C4
Illingworth Pl. MK6	23 E2
INDUSTRIAL ESTATES:	
Blakelands Ind Est. MK14	14 B1
Bleak Hall Ind Est. MK6	23 E5
Bletchley Park Training Centre. MK3	29 G4
Brinklow Ind Est. MK10	25 F2
Crownhill Ind Est. MK8	17 F6
Denbigh East Ind Est. MK1	30 B3
Denbigh Hall Ind Est. MK3	29 F1
Denbigh West Ind Est. MK1	29 G3
Fenny Lock Ind Est. MK1	30 C3
Fox Milne Ind Est. MK15	20 C3
Kiln Farm Ind Est. MK11	16 C2
Kingston Ind Est. MK10	21 G6
Knowlhill Ind Est. MK5	22 C4
Linford Wood Ind Est. MK14	19 E2
Mountfarm Ind Est. MK1	30 B1
Northfield Ind Est. MK15	20 D3
Redmoor Ind Est. MK6	23 F6
Rooksley Ind Est. MK13	18 B5
Shenley Wood Ind Est. MK5	22 A5
Snelshall West Ind Est. MK4	28 A6
Stacey Bushes Ind Est. MK12	17 E1
Tilbrook Ind Est. MK7	31 F1
Tongwell Ind Est. MK15	14 D3
Winterhill Ind Est. MK5	22 D3
Wymbush Ind Est. MK8	17 F3
Ingleton Clo. MK13	18 C4
Innholder Ct. MK14	19 F2
Inverness Clo. MK3	29 E3
Ireland Clo. MK7	25 G6
Ironmonger Ct. MK14	19 F2
Irving Dale. MK7	25 H5
Isaacson Dri. MK7	25 G4
Islingbrook. MK5	28 B1

43

Ivy Clo. MK16 — 9 F3
Ivy La. MK17 — 32 A5

Jacobs Clo. MK14 — 13 G4
Jamaica. MK6 — 23 F4
James Way. MK1 — 29 H3
Japonica La. MK15 — 14 D5
Jeeves Clo. MK6 — 23 H3
Jenkins Clo. MK5 — 26 F2
Jennings. MK14 — 13 F4
Jersey St. MK12 — 11 H3
Johnston Pl. MK6 — 5 F6
Jonathans. MK6 — 23 F3
Joules Ct. MK5 — 22 C5
Juniper Gdns. MK7 — 25 F3

Kalman Gdns. MK7 — 25 G5
Kaplan Clo. MK5 — 22 B5
Katherine Clo. MK7 — 25 E6
Katrine Pl. MK2 — 33 G3
Keasden Ct. MK4 — 28 B3
Keats Clo. MK16 — 9 B2
Keats Way. MK3 — 32 D1
Kellan Dri. MK6 — 23 F1
Kelso Clo. MK3 — 32 B2
Kelvin Dri. MK5 — 22 C4
Kemble Ct. MK15 — 19 G2
Kempton Gdns. MK3 — 32 B2
Kenchester. MK13 — 17 G1
Kenilworth Dri. MK3 — 29 E5
Kennet Dri. MK3 — 29 E4
Kennington Clo. MK16 — 9 C3
Kensington Dri. MK8 — 17 F4
Kents Rd. MK14 — 13 G3
Kenwell Ct. MK15 — 20 A5
Kenwood Gate. MK6 — 19 G5
Keppel Av. MK19 — 12 B1
Kepwick. MK8 — 17 F4
Kercheron Pl. MK14 — 19 E3
Kercroft. MK8 — 17 E3
Kernow Cres. MK6 — 5 H5
Kerria Pl. MK3 — 29 F2
Kersey. MK14 — 13 F4
Ketelbey Nook. MK7 — 25 H5
Ketton Clo. MK15 — 15 E4
Kew Ct. MK8 — 17 G4
Keynes Clo. MK16 — 9 F2
Khasaberry. MK7 — 25 F5
Kidd Clo. MK8 — 26 E1
Kildonan Pl. MK12 — 16 C2
Kiln Farm Ind Est. MK11 — 16 C2
Kilwinning Dri. MK10 — 24 D1
Kimbolton Ct. MK14 — 14 B3
Kincardine Dri. MK3 — 29 E2
Kindermann Ct. MK5 — 22 B5
Kindleton. MK14 — 14 A3
King Edward St. MK13 — 12 C4
King George Cres. MK11 — 10 D3
King St. MK11 — 10 D4
Kingsbridge. MK4 — 28 D2
Kingsfold. MK13 — 13 E4
Kingscoe Leys. MK10 — 21 E5
Kingsley Clo. MK16 — 9 A2
Kingston Av. MK11 — 10 D4
Kingston Ind Est. MK10 — 25 G1
Kinloch Pl. MK2 — 33 H3
Kinnear Clo. MK8 — 17 E6
Kinross Dri. MK3 — 29 E3
Kipling Dri. MK16 — 9 A2
Kipling Rd. MK3 — 33 E1
Kirke Clo. MK5 — 22 A5
Kirkeby Clo. MK14 — 13 G5
Kirkham Ct. MK5 — 4 B6
Kirkstall Pl. MK6 — 5 E6
Kirtlington. MK15 — 19 G2
Kite Hill. MK6 — 23 G2
Knapp Gate. MK5 — 17 G6
Knebworth Gate. MK14 — 14 B2
Knowl Gate. MK5 — 22 C3
Knowles Grn. MK2 — 30 A5
Knowlhill Ind Est. MK5 — 25 E2
Knox Bridge. MK7 — 25 E2
Krypton Clo. MK5 — 22 B4

Laburnum Gro. MK2 — 30 C5

Lacy Dri. MK15 — 14 C4
Lady Mead Clo. MK17 — 27 B7
Laggan Ct. MK2 — 33 H4
Lagonda Clo. MK16 — 9 F2
Laidon Clo. MK2 — 33 H4
Laker Ct. MK6 — 23 E3
Lakes La. MK16 — 9 B1
Lakeside Gro. MK7 — 30 D1
Lamb Clo. MK16 — 9 A2
Lamb La. MK7 — 25 F3
Lamberhurst Gro. MK7 — 25 E3
Lamberts Croft. MK12 — 11 H5
Lambourn Ct. MK4 — 28 C3
Lammas. MK6 — 23 G5
Lampitts Cross. MK6 — 23 G4
Lamport Ct. MK8 — 17 G5
Lamva Ct. MK11 — 11 E5
Lancaster Gate. MK3 — 29 E6
Landrace Ct. MK5 — 26 F4
Landsborough Gate.
  MK15 — 14 D4
Lanercost Cres. MK10 — 21 G6
Lanfranc Gdns. MK15 — 14 C4
Langcliffe Dri. MK13 — 18 B3
Langdale Clo. MK2 — 33 G4
Langerstone La. MK4 — 28 B4
Langford Pl. MK7 — 31 E2
Langland Rd. MK6 — 24 A4
Langton Dri. MK8 — 17 E3
Lanthorn Clo. MK14 — 19 E1
Larch Gro. MK2 — 30 B6
Larkin Clo. MK16 — 9 A1
Larkspur Av. MK14 — 19 E3
Larwood Pl. MK6 — 5 G6
Lasborough Rd. MK10 — 21 G6
Lascelles Clo. MK15 — 14 C4
Laser Clo. MK5 — 22 C4
Lastingham Gro. MK4 — 28 B2
Latimer. MK11 — 10 D5
Launceston Ct. MK5 — 22 B4
Launde. MK10 — 21 E6
Laurel Clo. MK8 — 26 D1
Lavender Gro. MK7 — 25 E5
Lawns Mead Gdns. MK16 — 9 D2
Lawson Pl. MK5 — 22 B5
Leaberry. MK13 — 13 E3
Leafield Rise. MK8 — 17 E4
Leary Cres. MK16 — 9 F3
Leasowe Pl. MK13 — 4 B2
Ledbury. MK14 — 13 G3
Leigh Hill. MK4 — 28 B4
*Lenborough Ct,
  Pattison La. MK15 — 20 A6
Lennon Dri. MK8 — 26 E1
Lennox Rd. MK2 — 30 B5
Lenthall Clo. MK13 — 17 G1
Leominster Gate. MK10 — 24 D1
Leon Av. MK2 — 30 B5
Leonardslee. MK4 — 27 F5
Leopard Dri. MK15 — 14 B4
Lester Ct. MK7 — 25 G3
Leven Clo. MK2 — 33 G3
Lewis Clo. MK16 — 9 A2
Leyland Pl. MK6 — 5 F6
Leys Rd. MK5 — 22 B5
Lichfield Down. MK7 — 25 E5
Lightfoot Ct. MK7 — 24 D5
Lilac Clo. MK17 — 32 A5
Lilleshall Av. MK10 — 24 D1
Limbaud Clo. MK7 — 25 E5
Lime Clo. MK16 — 9 C3
Lincesdale Gro. MK5 — 4 A5
Lincoln. MK14 — 13 F3
Linden Gro. MK14 — 13 H3
Lindisfarne Dri. MK10 — 21 E6
Lindores Croft. MK10 — 25 F1
Linford Av. MK16 — 9 B3
Linford La,
  Willen. MK15 — 15 E4
Linford La,
  Woolstone. MK15 — 20 A4
Linford Wood Ind Est.
  MK14 — 19 E2
Lingfield. MK12 — 17 E1

Lintlaw Pl. MK3 — 29 F2
Linton Clo. MK13 — 18 C3
Lipscomb La. MK5 — 22 A3
Lissel Rd. MK6 — 24 C5
Little Cote. MK8 — 17 G4
Little Dunmow. MK10 — 21 E6
Little Habton. MK4 — 28 B2
Little Hame. MK10 — 20 D4
Little Linford La. MK16 — 9 A3
Little Meadow. MK5 — 22 B3
Little Stanton. MK14 — 13 G4
Little Stocking. MK5 — 28 A1
Littlemere. MK8 — 17 E4
Livesey Hill. MK5 — 22 B3
Livingstone Dri. MK15 — 20 A3
Lloyds. MK6 — 23 F3
Lock View La. MK1 — 30 C3
Lockton Ct. MK4 — 28 B2
Lodge Farm Ct. MK19 — 8 C1
Lodge Gate. MK14 — 13 H4
Lomond Dri. MK2 — 33 G5
London End. MK17 — 32 B4
London End La. MK17 — 31 G3
London Rd. MK10 — 21 E3
London Rd. MK11 — 10 D4
London Rd. MK16 — 15 G1
London Rd. MK19 — 10 B2
Long Ayres. MK7 — 31 E2
Longcross. MK15 — 14 B5
Longfellow Dri. MK16 — 9 B2
Longhedge. MK7 — 31 E2
Longleat Ct. MK8 — 17 G5
Longpeak Clo. MK4 — 28 B4
Longville. MK12 — 11 F2
Lords Clo. MK2 — 30 A4
Loriner Pl. MK14 — 19 F2
Loseley Ct. MK8 — 17 G4
Lothersdale. MK13 — 18 B2
Lothian Clo. MK3 — 29 E3
Loughton Rd. MK13 — 17 H1
Lovat St. MK16 — 9 D2
Lovatt Dri. MK3 — 28 D5
Lower Eighth St. MK9 — 5 F3
Lower Fourth St. MK9 — 4 D4
Lower Ninth St. MK9 — 5 F3
Lower Second St. MK9 — 4 C5
Lower Stone Hayes.
  MK14 — 14 A4
Lower Tenth St. MK9 — 5 F3
Lower Third St. MK9 — 4 D5
Lower Twelfth St. MK9 — 5 G2
Lowland Rd. MK4 — 28 B4
Lowndes Gro. MK5 — 17 G6
Loxbeare Dri. MK4 — 28 C1
Lucas Pl. MK6 — 24 B2
Luccombe. MK4 — 28 D2
Lucy La. MK5 — 22 B2
Ludgate. MK6 — 23 E3
Ludgate. MK6 — 23 E3
Ludholme. MK13 — 18 B3
Ludlow Clo. MK3 — 29 E5
Lufford Pk. MK14 — 14 A3
Lullingstone Dri. MK13 — 12 C6
Luxborough Gro. MK4 — 22 C6
Luttlemarsh. MK7 — 24 D5
Lutyens Gro. MK7 — 25 G5
Lydiard. MK8 — 17 F5
Lynmouth Cres. MK4 — 28 C1
Lynott Clo. MK8 — 26 E1
Lyon Rd. MK1 — 29 G2

Maclaren Ct. MK6 — 23 F2
Magdalen Clo. MK11 — 10 C3
Magenta Clo. MK3 — 33 G2
Magpie Clo. MK5 — 22 B6
Mahler Clo. MK7 — 25 F5
Maidenhead Av. MK13 — 4 B2
Maidstone Rd. MK10 — 21 F5
Main St. MK19 — 8 B6
Malbons Ct. MK6 — 23 E3
Malins Gate. MK14 — 13 H3
Malletts Clo. MK11 — 10 D4
Mallow Gate. MK14 — 5 E1
Malvern Dri. MK11 — 11 E5

Mandeville Dri. MK10 — 21 F6
Manifold La. MK5 — 28 A2
Manor Clo. MK10 — 20 D5
Manor Clo. MK19 — 8 A5
Manor Dri. MK19 — 12 B1
Manor Rd. MK12 — 11 G2
Manor Rd. MK16 — 9 B3
Manor Rd. MK17 — 32 B5
Manor Rd. MK2 — 30 B6
Manorfields Rd. MK19 — 10 A3
Manse Clo. MK11 — 10 C3
Mansel Clo. MK19 — 8 A5
Mansell Clo. MK5 — 22 A4
Manshead Ct. MK11 — 11 E4
Maple Dean. MK12 — 17 E1
Maple Durham. MK7 — 31 E2
Maple Gro. MK2 — 30 C5
March Mdw. MK7 — 25 G3
Maree Clo. MK2 — 33 G3
Marigold Pl. MK14 — 18 D3
Marina Dri. MK12 — 12 A6
Marjoram Pl. MK14 — 18 D3
Market Hill. MK6 — 23 H2
Market Sq. MK11 — 10 C4
Marlborough Gate. MK9 — 5 G1
Marlborough St,
  Milton Keynes. MK14 — 19 E1
Marlborough St,
  Stantonbury. MK14 — 13 F3
Marlborough St. MK6 — 24 A3
Marlborough St. MK9 — 19 F4
Marley Gro. MK8 — 26 E1
Marlow Dri. MK16 — 9 A2
Marram Clo. MK6 — 23 G5
Marron La. MK12 — 11 H4
Marsh Dri. MK14 — 14 A1
Marsh End Rd. MK16 — 9 D2
Marshalls La. MK15 — 20 A5
Marshaw Pl. MK4 — 28 B3
Marshworth. MK6 — 24 B4
Martin Clo. MK14 — 19 E1
Martingale Pl. MK14 — 19 F3
Marwood Clo. MK4 — 28 C2
Maryland Rd. MK15 — 14 C3
Masefield Clo. MK16 — 9 B3
Masefield Gro. MK3 — 33 E1
Maslin Dri. MK6 — 23 G5
Mason. MK14 — 13 F3
Massie Clo. MK15 — 14 C5
Mathiesen Rd. MK13 — 12 D5
Matilda Gdns. MK5 — 22 B5
Matthew Ct. MK5 — 22 B4
Maudsley Clo. MK5 — 22 B4
Maulden Gdns. MK14 — 14 B3
Maxham. MK5 — 28 A2
Mayditch Pl. MK13 — 4 B1
Mayer Gdns. MK5 — 22 C5
Maynard Clo. MK13 — 17 H2
McConnell Dri. MK12 — 12 B4
Meadow La. MK10 — 21 E5
Meadow Sweet. MK7 — 25 F5
Meads Clo. MK13 — 13 E3
Medale Rd. MK6 — 23 G5
Medes Well. MK4 — 29 E1
Medhurst. MK8 — 17 E3
Medland. MK6 — 24 B3
Medway Clo. MK16 — 9 E3
Melbourne Ter. MK13 — 12 D4
Melfort Dri. MK2 — 33 G4
Melick Rd. MK6 — 23 G6
Melrose Av. MK3 — 29 F2
Melton. MK14 — 13 F3
Mendelssohn Gro. MK7 — 25 G6
Menteith Clo. MK2 — 33 G3
Mentmore Ct. MK8 — 17 F5
Menzies Ct. MK5 — 22 B6
Mercers Dri. MK13 — 13 E5
Mercury Gro. MK8 — 26 E1
Meriland Ct. MK2 — 33 H4
Merlewood Dri. MK4 — 26 E3
Mersey Clo. MK3 — 28 D4
Mersey Way. MK3 — 28 D4
Merthen Gro. MK4 — 28 B4
Merton Dri. MK6 — 23 G6

Quince Clo. MK7   25 F5
Quinton Dri. MK13   17 H2

Rackstraw Gro. MK7   25 H5
Radcliffe St. MK12   12 A5
Radman Gro. MK12   11 F4
Radworthy. MK4   28 C1
Rainbow Dri. MK6   23 F3
Rainsborough. MK14   14 B3
Ramsay Clo. MK13   17 H2
Ramsgill Ct. MK13   18 B3
Ramsoms Av. MK14   19 E4
Ramsthorn Gro. MK7   25 E4
Randolph Clo. MK13   12 D5
Ranelagh Gdns. MK16   9 D4
Rangers Ct. MK3   17 F5
Rannoch Clo. MK2   33 G3
Rashleigh Pl. MK6   22 D3
Rathbone Clo. MK8   17 E6
Ravel Clo. MK7   25 H4
Ravensbourne Pl. MK6   19 G5
Ravenscar Ct. MK4   28 B3
Ravigill Pl. MK12   17 E1
Rawlins Rd. MK13   17 H1
Rayleigh Clo. MK5   22 A4
Rectory Fields. MK15   20 A5
Rectory Rd. MK19   12 D1
Red House Clo. MK17   32 B4
Redbourne Ct. MK11   11 E4
Redbridge. MK14   13 G4
Redcote Manor. MK7   24 D6
Redding Gro. MK8   26 E1
Redhuish Clo. MK4   28 D1
Redland Dri. MK5   22 B3
Redmoor Ind Est. MK6   23 F6
Redvers Gate. MK15   14 C4
Redwood Gate. MK5   22 B6
Reeves Croft. MK12   16 D1
Regent St. MK4   30 A4
Rendlesham. MK15   20 A5
Rhodes Pl. MK6   23 E3
Rhondda Clo. MK1   30 C3
Rhoscolyn Dri. MK4   28 B5
Rhuddlan Clo. MK5   17 G6
Ribble Clo. MK16   9 E3
Ribble Cres. MK3   28 D4
Richardson Pl. MK6   5 F5
Richborough. MK13   12 D5
Richmond Clo. MK3   28 D4
Richmond Way. MK16   9 D3
Rickley La. MK3   29 F4
Rickyard Clo. MK13   17 G1
Ridgeway. MK11   11 E5
Ridgeway. MK12   11 F4
Rika Ct. MK7   25 F5
Rillington Gdns. MK4   28 B2
Rimsdale Ct. MK2   33 G5
Ring Rd East. MK7   24 D4
Ring Rd North. MK7   24 C3
Ring Rd West. MK7   24 C3
River Clo. MK16   9 D2
Rivercrest Rd. MK19   10 B2
Riverside. MK7   9 E2
Rixband Clo. MK7   25 E6
Robertson Clo. MK5   17 G6
Robins Hill. MK6   23 G4
Robson Pl. MK8   17 E6
Roche Gdns. MK3   29 F4
Rochester Ct. MK5   22 A5
Rochfords. MK6   23 F3
Rockingham Dri. MK14   19 E2
Rockspray Gro. MK7   25 E5
Rodwell Gdns. MK7   25 G6
Roebuck Way. MK5   22 C4
Roeburn Cres. MK4   28 B3
Rogers Croft. MK6   24 B3
Rolvenden Gro. MK7   25 F3
Rooksley Ind Est. MK13   18 B5
Rosebay Clo. MK7   25 F5
Rosecomb Pl. MK5   22 A6
Rosemary Ct. MK7   25 E5
Rosemullion Av. MK4   28 B4
Roslyn Ct. MK15   15 E4
Ross Way. MK3   29 E2

Rossal Pl. MK12   16 D1
Rossendale. MK14   13 G4
Rossini Pl. MK7   25 H5
Rothersthorpe. MK14   14 B3
Roveley Ct. MK11   11 E5
Rowan Dri. MK19   12 B1
Rowlands Clo. MK2   30 C4
Rowle Clo. MK14   13 G4
Rowsham Dell. MK14   14 A1
Rubbra Clo. MK7   25 G5
Rudchesters. MK13   12 D6
Runford Ct. MK5   22 C5
Runnymede. MK14   14 B2
Rushleys Clo. MK5   17 G6
Rushmere Clo. MK17   31 G3
Rushton Ct. MK8   17 F5
Ruskin Ct. MK16   9 D4
Rusland Circus. MK4   28 C2
Russell St. MK11   10 C4
Rutherford Gate. MK5   22 C5
Ruthven Clo. MK2   33 G4
Rydal Way. MK2   33 G3
Ryecroft. MK4   29 E1
Ryeland. MK11   10 D3
Rylstone Clo. MK13   18 B4
Ryton Pl. MK4   28 B2

Saddington. MK6   24 B4
Saddlers Pl. MK14   19 G2
Saffron Ct. MK2   33 G1
St Aidans Clo. MK3   32 C2
St Andrews Rd. MK3   32 C1
St Antonys Pl. MK4   28 B5
St Bees. MK10   25 E1
St Botolphs. MK10   25 E1
St Brides Clo. MK6   19 H5
St Catherines Av. MK3   32 B2
St Clements Dri. MK3   32 B2
St Davids Rd. MK3   32 C2
St Dunstans. MK6   23 F3
St Faiths Clo. MK17   32 B5
St Georges Rd. MK3   32 B2
St Georges Way. MK12   12 B4
St Giles Mews. MK11   10 C3
St Giles St. MK13   12 C4
St Govans Clo. MK4   28 B5
St James St. MK13   12 C4
St John St. MK16   9 E2
St Johns Cres. MK12   12 A6
St Johns Rd. MK3   32 B2
St Lawrence Vw. MK13   17 G2
St Leger Ct. MK14   13 H3
St Leger Dri. MK14   13 G3
St Margarets Clo. MK16   9 E3
St Margarets Ct. MK2   30 B5
St Martins St. MK2   30 A4
St Mary St. MK13   12 C4
St Marys Av. MK11   10 D4
St Marys Av. MK3   32 C1
St Marys Clo. MK7   25 H3
St Matthews Ct. MK3   32 C2
St Michaels Dri. MK7   24 D3
St Patricks Rd. MK3   32 C2
St Pauls Ct. MK11   10 C3
St Pauls Rd. MK3   32 B2
St Pauls Yd. MK16   9 D3
St Peters Way. MK13   12 D3
St Stephens Dri. MK15   14 D4
St Thomas Ct. MK4   27 F6
Salden Clo. MK5   22 B4
Salford Rd. MK17   21 G4
Salisbury Gro. MK14   14 A1
Salters Mews. MK14   19 E1
Samphire Ct. MK7   25 E4
Sandal Ct. MK5   22 A5
Sandbrier Clo. MK7   25 E4
Sandown Ct. MK3   32 B2
Sandringham Pl. MK2   30 A5
Sandwell Ct. MK8   16 D3
Sandy Clo. MK14   13 G3
Sandywell Dri. MK15   19 G2
Santen Gro. MK2   33 H4
Saracens Wharf. MK2   30 C4
Saunders Clo. MK7   25 G4

Saxon Gate. MK9   5 E2
Saxon St. MK2   30 A5
Saxon St. MK1   30 A1
Saxon St. MK13   18 C2
Saxon St,
   Milton Keynes. MK6   5 F5
Saxon St,
   Oldbrook. MK6   23 E1
Scardale. MK13   18 B2
Scatterill Clo. MK13   17 H1
School Dri. MK17   32 A5
School La. MK19   8 C2
School La. MK5   22 B2
School St. MK13   12 D4
Schumann Clo. MK7   25 G6
Scotch Firs. MK7   25 G4
Scotney Gdns. MK3   29 E5
Scott Dri. MK16   9 B2
Scriven Ct. MK15   15 F4
Seagrave Ct. MK7   24 D6
Secklow Gate. MK9   5 F1
Second Av. MK1   29 H3
Sedgemere. MK8   17 E4
Selbourne Av. MK3   32 C1
Selby Gro. MK5   22 A5
Selkirk Gro. MK3   29 F2
Selworthy. MK4   28 D1
Serjeants Grn. MK14   19 F1
Serles Clo. MK6   23 G4
Serpentine Ct. MK2   33 G3
Severn Dri. MK16   9 E3
Severn Way. MK3   28 D4
Shackleton Pl. MK6   5 F5
Shaftesbury Cres. MK3   29 F3
Shakespeare Clo. MK16   9 A1
Shamrock Clo. MK7   25 F4
Shannon Ct. MK14   19 F2
Sharkham Ct. MK4   28 B4
Sharman Way. MK13   17 G2
Shaw Clo. MK16   9 A2
Shearmans. MK11   11 F5
Sheepcoat Clo. MK5   22 A5
Sheldon Ct. MK8   17 F4
Shelley Clo. MK16   9 B2
Shelley Dri. MK3   32 D1
Shellin Gro. MK2   33 H4
Shelsmore. MK14   14 B3
Shenley Rd. MK17   27 C7
Shenley Rd. MK3   29 E4
Shenley Rd. MK5   22 A3
Shenley Wood Ind Est.
   MK5   22 A6
Sheperds Gro. MK5   26 F1
Shepherds. MK11   11 F5
Sheppards Clo. MK16   9 C3
Shepperton Clo. MK19   8 B3
Sherbourne Dri. MK7   31 F1
Sherington Rd. MK16   9 E1
Shernfold. MK7   25 E3
Sherwood Dri. MK3   29 G3
Shilling Clo. MK15   14 B4
Shipley Rd. MK16   9 B3
Shipman Ct. MK15   14 D4
Shipton Hill. MK13   13 E5
Shire Ct. MK14   19 F2
Shirlby La. MK5   22 A4
Shirley Moor. MK7   25 F2
Shirwell Cres. MK4   22 C5
Shoreham Rise. MK8   17 E4
Shuttleworth Gro. MK7   25 G4
Sidlaw Ct. MK11   11 E5
Silbury Arc. MK9   5 E3
Silbury Blvd. MK9   4 C4
Silicon Ct. MK5   22 C5
Silver St. MK11   10 C4
Silver St. MK16   9 D3
Silverweed Ct. MK7   25 F4
Simnel. MK6   23 G4
Simons Bath. MK4   28 D3
Simons Lea. MK13   17 H2
Simpson. MK6   24 C5
Simpson Dri. MK6   24 C5
Simpson Rd. MK7   24 D5
Sinclair Ct. MK1   29 G2

Sipthorp Clo. MK7   25 G4
Sitwell Clo. MK16   9 A1
Skeats Wharf. MK15   14 C4
Skeldon Gate. MK9   19 F3
Skene Clo. MK2   33 G4
Skipton Clo. MK15   14 D5
Slade La. MK11   11 E5
Slated Row. MK12   11 F2
Smarbridge Walk. MK15   15 E4
Smarden Bell. MK7   25 E2
Smeaton Clo. MK14   14 B1
Smithergill Ct. MK13   18 B3
Snaith Cres. MK5   22 B3
Snelshall St. MK4   28 A5
Snelshall West Ind Est.
   MK4   28 A6
Snowberry Clo. MK12   17 E1
Snowdon Dri. MK6   22 D2
Snowshill Clo. MK14   14 A1
Sokeman Clo. MK12   11 F4
Solar Ct. MK14   13 H3
Somerset Clo. MK3   29 E5
Sorrell Dri. MK16   9 A2
Soskin Dri. MK14   13 G5
South Eighth St. MK9   5 F4
South Fifth St. MK9   5 E5
South Lawne. MK3   29 F5
South Ninth St. MK9   5 F4
South Row. MK9   5 E5
South Seventh St. MK9   5 E4
South Sixth St. MK9   5 E4
South St. MK19   8 C2
South Tenth St. MK9   5 G3
South Ter. MK2   30 A4
Southbridge Gro. MK7   25 E3
Southern Way. MK12   12 A6
Southfield Clo. MK15   15 E4
Southside. MK10   20 D6
Southwick Ct. MK8   17 F5
Soveriegn Dri. MK15   14 B4
Spark Way. MK16   9 A2
Sparsholt Clo. MK4   28 C3
Spearmint Clo. MK7   25 F5
Specklands. MK5   17 G6
Speedwell Pl. MK14   19 E4
Speldhurst Ct. MK7   25 F3
Spencer. MK14   13 F3
Spenlows Rd. MK3   29 F2
Spoonley Wood. MK13   12 C6
Springfield Blvd. MK6   19 G6
Squires Clo. MK6   23 G4
Stacey Av. MK12   12 B5
Stacey Bushes Ind Est.
   MK12   17 E1
Stafford Gro. MK5   22 B4
Stainton Dri. MK13   18 C4
Stamford Av. MK6   19 G6
Stanbridge Ct. MK11   10 D4
Standing Way. MK3   29 E2
Standing Way. MK6   23 F6
Standing Way. MK6   24 A3
Standing Way. MK7   25 E1
Stanmore Gdns. MK16   9 C4
Stanton Av. MK13   13 E5
Stanton Gate. MK14   13 G3
Stantonbury Clo. MK13   12 D3
Stanway Clo. MK15   19 G2
Staplehall Rd. MK1   30 B3
Staters Pound. MK15   14 B5
Statham Pl. MK6   5 G6
Station Rd. MK16   9 D2
Station Rd. MK17   31 F3
Station Rd. MK19   8 B2
Stavordale. MK10   25 E1
Stedward Clo. MK14   19 E1
Steinbeck Cres. MK4   27 F8
Sterling Clo. MK15   14 B5
Stevens Fld. MK7   25 G4
Stock La. MK17   27 B6
Stockdale. MK13   18 B2
Stockwell La. MK5   25 H2
Stoke Rd. MK17   32 B4
Stoke Rd. MK2   33 H2
Stokenchurch Pl. MK13   4 C1

Entry	Ref
Stone Hill. MK8	17 E4
Stonecrop Pl. MK14	19 E4
Stonegate. MK14	12 D6
Stoneleigh Ct. MK5	27 E5
Stonor Ct. MK8	17 G5
Stotfold Ct. MK11	10 D5
Stour Clo. MK16	9 F3
Stour Clo. MK8	29 E4
Stourhead Gate. MK	27 E5
Stowe Ct. MK14	13 F3
Strangford Dri. MK2	33 G4
Stratfield Ct. MK8	17 G4
Stratford Rd. MK12	11 E3
Stratford Rd. MK17	27 A5
Stratford Rd, Cosgrove. MK19	8 A6
Stratford Rd, Upper Weald. MK19	16 B6
Strathnaver Pl. MK12	16 D1
Strauss Gro. MK7	25 G6
Streatham Pl. MK13	4 B3
Strudwick Dri. MK6	23 E2
Stuart Clo. MK2	30 B4
Studley Knapp. MK7	25 F4
Sturges Clo. MK7	24 D5
Suffolk Clo. MK3	29 F4
Sulgrave Ct. MK8	17 G5
Sullivan Cres. MK7	25 G5
Sultan Croft. MK5	22 A6
Summergill Ct. MK13	18 C3
Summerhayes. MK14	14 A4
Summerson Rd. MK6	23 F5
Sumner Ct. MK5	17 G6
Sunbury Clo. MK13	12 D5
Sunningdale Way. MK3	28 D4
Sunridge Clo. MK16	9 C4
Sunrise Parkway. MK14	18 D2
Sunset Clo. MK2	30 A5
Surrey Pl. MK3	29 E3
Surrey Rd. MK3	29 E3
Sussex Rd. MK3	29 E4
Sutcliffe Av. MK6	5 E5
Sutherland Gro. MK3	29 E2
Sutleye Ct. MK5	22 A5
Sutton Clo. MK4	28 B4
Swallowfield. MK8	17 F5
Swayne Rise. MK10	21 E4
Sweetlands Cnr. MK7	25 E2
Swift Clo. MK16	9 B2
Swimbridge La. MK4	28 D1
Swinden Clo. MK13	17 H1
Swinden Ct. MK13	18 B3
Sycamore Av. MK2	30 C5
Sykes Croft. MK4	28 B3
Symington Ct. MK5	22 B5
Syon Gdns. MK16	9 C4
Tabard Gdns. MK16	9 D4
Tacknell Dri. MK5	26 F3
Tadmarton. MK15	19 G2
Tadmere. MK8	17 E4
Talbot Ct. MK15	20 A6
Talland Av. MK6	5 G5
Tallis La. MK7	25 G5
Tamarisk Ct. MK7	25 F5
Tamworth Stubb. MK7	25 F3
Tandra. MK6	23 G5
Tanners Dri. MK14	14 B1
Tansman La. MK7	25 G5
Taranis Clo. MK7	25 F3
Tarbert Clo. MK4	33 G3
Tarnbrook Clo. MK4	28 B2
Tarragon Clo. MK7	25 E4
Tatling Gro. MK7	25 E4
Tattam Clo. MK15	20 A6
Tattenhoe La. MK3	28 C4
Tattenhoe St. MK4	28 A3
Tattersall Clo. MK5	22 A4
Taunton Deane. MK4	28 C3
Tavelhurst. MK8	17 F4
Taverner Clo. MK7	25 H5
Tavistock St. MK2	30 A4
Tay Rd. MK3	28 D4
Taylors Mews. MK14	19 E2
Teasel Av. MK14	18 D3
Tees Way. MK3	28 D4
Teign Clo. MK16	9 E3
Telford Way. MK14	14 C2
Temple. MK14	13 F4
Temple Clo. MK3	28 D6
Tene Acres. MK5	26 F2
Tennyson Dri. MK16	9 B2
Tennyson Gro. MK3	32 D1
Tenterden Cres. MK7	25 E3
Tewkesbury La. MK10	24 D1
Thames Clo. MK3	28 D5
Thames Dri. MK6	9 F3
Thane Ct. MK14	13 F4
The Approach. MK8	17 E3
The Beeches. MK1	30 B3
The Boundary. MK6	23 F2
The Canons. MK16	9 F3
The Carne. MK11	10 D4
The Chase. MK17	32 B4
The Chequers. MK19	8 B2
The Close. MK13	17 H1
The Craven. MK13	18 B4
The Crescent. MK19	12 B1
The Crescent. MK2	30 A4
The Elms. MK3	29 F5
The Fleet. MK6	19 H5
The Green. MK16	9 D3
The Green. MK19	8 B5
The Green. MK5	22 A2
The Green. MK6	24 A2
The Greys. MK6	24 A2
The Grove. MK13	17 G1
The Grove. MK16	9 C3
The Grove. MK3	29 F5
The Hedge Rows. MK4	29 E1
The Hide. MK6	23 H4
The High St. MK8	16 D4
The Homestead. MK5	22 A4
The Hooke. MK15	15 E4
The Hythe. MK8	17 E3
The Laurels. MK1	30 B3
The Limes. MK11	10 D5
The Limes. MK2	30 C5
The Linx. MK3	29 G2
The Lodge Park. MK16	9 C2
The Meadway. MK5	22 A3
The Mount. MK6	24 C6
The Nortons. MK7	31 E2
The Oval. MK6	23 E3
The Slade. MK17	32 B4
The Spinney. MK13	17 G1
The Square. MK12	12 A5
The Stocks. MK19	8 B6
The Wharf. MK14	14 A1
The Wharf. MK2	30 C6
Third Av. MK1	29 H3
Thirlmere Av. MK2	33 G2
Thirsk Gdns. MK3	32 A2
Thomas Dri. MK16	9 B1
Thompson St. MK13	12 D3
Thorncliffe. MK8	16 D4
Thorneycroft La. MK15	19 G2
Thornley Croft. MK4	28 C3
Thorwold Pl. MK5	22 B4
Thresher Gro. MK12	11 F4
Thrupp Clo. MK19	8 C2
Thurne Clo. MK16	9 F3
Thursby Clo. MK15	15 E4
Thyne Clo. MK16	9 A2
Tickford St. MK16	9 E2
Tiffany Clo. MK2	33 G2
Tilbrook Ind Est. MK7	31 F1
Tilers Rd. MK11	16 C3
Tillman Clo. MK12	11 G4
Timbers Combe. MK4	28 D1
Timbold Dri. MK7	24 D2
Tintagel Ct. MK6	5 H6
Tippett Clo. MK7	25 G6
Titchmarsh Ct. MK6	23 E2
Tolcarne Av. MK6	23 G1
Tongwell Ind Est. MK15	14 D3
Tongwell La. MK16	9 D4
Tongwell St. MK10	20 D4
Tongwell St, Fox Milne. MK15	20 C3
Tongwell St, Willen. MK15	15 E3
Tongwell St. MK7	25 F2
Tongwell Way. MK7	25 G5
Top Meadow. MK7	31 E1
Torre Clo. MK3	29 F3
Torridon Ct. MK2	33 G4
Towan Av. MK6	23 F2
Towcester Rd. MK19	10 A2
Tower Cres. MK14	19 F1
Tower Dri. MK14	19 E1
Townsend Gro. MK13	13 E3
Trafalgar Av. MK3	28 D3
Translands Brigg. MK13	18 B4
Travell Ct. MK13	17 H2
Travis Gro. MK3	29 F5
Treborough. MK4	28 C2
Tredington Gro. MK7	31 E1
Tremayne Ct. MK6	5 H6
Trent Dri. MK16	9 E3
Trent Rd. MK3	29 E4
Trentishoe Cres. MK4	28 D2
Tresham Ct. MK5	17 G6
Trevithick La. MK5	22 B5
Trevone Ct. MK6	5 H6
Trinity Rd. MK12	11 F2
Trispen Ct. MK6	5 H6
Trout Beck. MK6	23 H2
Trubys Gdns. MK6	23 F3
Trueman Pl. MK6	23 E2
Trumpton La. MK7	25 G3
Tudeley Hale. MK7	25 F2
Tudor Gdns. MK11	10 D5
Tuffnell Clo. MK15	15 F4
Tulla Ct. MK2	33 G4
Tummel Way. MK2	33 G3
Tunbridge Gro. MK7	25 E2
Turnberry Clo. MK3	28 C6
Turnbridge. MK7	25 E2
Turners Mews. MK14	19 E1
Turneys Dri. MK12	11 E3
Turnmill Av. MK6	19 G5
Turpyn Ct. MK6	24 B2
Tweed Dri. MK3	28 D4
Twinflower. MK7	25 F4
Twitchen La. MK4	28 C2
Twyford La. MK7	25 F5
Tyburn Av. MK6	19 G5
Tylers Grn. MK13	4 C1
Tyrill. MK14	13 F4
Tyson Pl. MK6	23 E2
Ulverscroft. MK10	21 E6
Ulyett Pl. MK6	23 E2
Underwood Pl. MK6	23 E2
Union St. MK16	9 D2
Upper Fifth St. MK9	4 D3
Upper Fourth St. MK9	4 C4
Upper Second St. MK9	4 C4
Upper Stone Hayes. MK14	14 A4
Upper Third St. MK9	4 C4
Upton Gro. MK5	22 C5
Vache La. MK5	26 F2
Valens Clo. MK8	26 E1
Valentine Ct. MK8	17 E6
Valerian Pl. MK16	9 A2
Van Der Bilt Ct. MK13	12 C5
Vantage Ct. MK16	9 F3
Vauxhall. MK13	13 E5
Vellan Av. MK6	23 G1
Venables La. MK15	14 C4
Venetian Ct. MK7	25 G3
Verdi Clo. MK7	25 G5
Verdon Dri. MK15	14 C4
Verity Pl. MK6	5 G6
Verley Clo. MK6	24 A2
Vermont Pl. MK6	14 D2
Veryan Pl. MK6	19 G6
Vicarage Gdns. MK13	17 G2
Vicarage Rd. MK11	10 C3
Vicarage Rd. MK13	17 G2
Vicarage Rd. MK17	27 B7
Vicarage Rd. MK2	30 B4
Vicarage Walk. MK11	10 C3
Victoria Rd. MK2	30 B4
Victoria St. MK12	12 A5
Vienna Gro. MK8	12 C5
Vincent Av. MK8	17 F6
Vintners Mews. MK14	19 E1
Virginia. MK6	23 F3
Viscount Way. MK2	30 A4
Vyne Cres. MK8	17 G5
Wadesmill La. MK7	31 E1
Wadhurst La. MK7	25 E2
Wagner Clo. MK7	25 G6
Wainers Croft. MK12	11 G5
Wakefield Clo. MK14	19 E1
Walbank Gro. MK5	28 A2
Walbrook Av. MK6	19 G5
Walgrave Dri. MK13	17 H2
Walkhampton Av. MK13	4 A2
Wallace St. MK13	12 C4
Wallinger Dri. MK5	28 A2
Wallingford. MK13	13 E6
Wallmead Gdns. MK5	22 B3
Walney Pl. MK5	27 F6
Walnut Clo. MK16	9 B3
Walnut Dri. MK2	30 C5
Walshs Manor. MK14	13 G4
Walton Dri. MK7	24 D4
Walton End. MK7	25 G4
Walton Heath. MK3	28 D5
Walton Rd. MK6	24 C5
Walton Rd. MK10	20 D5
Walton Rd. MK17	25 H3
Walton Rd, Caldecotte. MK7	31 E1
Walton Rd, Walnut Tree. MK7	25 E4
Walton Rd, Wavendon Gate. MK7	25 G4
Wandlebury. MK14	14 B3
Wandsworth Pl. MK13	4 C2
Ward Rd. MK1	30 B2
Wardle Pl. MK6	22 D2
Wardstone End. MK4	28 B3
Warmington Gdns. MK15	19 G2
Warners Rd. MK17	32 B5
Warren Bank. MK6	24 C5
Warwick Rd. MK3	29 E5
Washfield. MK4	28 D2
Wastel. MK6	23 G5
Watchet Ct. MK4	28 D2
Water Eaton Rd. MK2	33 F1
Water House Clo. MK16	9 D2
Waterloo Ct. MK3	29 E3
Waterlow Clo. MK16	9 D4
Waterside. MK6	23 H1
Watersmeet Clo. MK4	28 D1
Watling Av. MK1	30 B3
Watling St, Kiln Farm. MK11	16 A2
Watling St, Stony Stratford. MK11	11 E5
Watling St. MK19	10 A1
Watling St. MK4	22 D5
Watling St. MK5	22 A3
Watling St. MK8	16 D4
Watling Ter. MK2	30 C4
Watten Ct. MK2	33 H4
Wavell Ct. MK15	14 C4
Waveney Clo. MK16	9 F3
Wealdstone Pl. MK6	19 G5
Weavers Hill. MK11	11 F6
Webber Heath. MK7	25 G6
Websters Mdw. MK4	28 B3
Wedgewood Av. MK14	14 B2
Welburn Gro. MK4	28 A2
Welland Dri. MK16	9 F3
Wellfield Ct. MK15	15 E4
Wellhayes. MK14	14 A4
Wenning La. MK4	28 A3

WOBURN SANDS

YARDLEY GOBION/ POTTERSPURY